The Key To Life
By
S.M.Holmes

SUMMARY

The aim of this book is to show that whatever religion you follow however much they contradict each other, they are in fact following the same basics beliefs. I am also making you aware of the fact that science and religion run alongside each other, showing that religion is a story version to help us understand the scientific facts that have been proven. Spiritualism is a common sense religion, one of knowing and living. Accepting all truths and endeavouring to prove their validity. Truths are found in nature, in other religions, in writings, in science, in philosophy, in divine law, and are received through spirit communication, everything is connected whether it be, religion, spirituality, philosophy or scientific beliefs. We are all one, we all have free will. They are all searching for the same truth. We are all searching for the same truth... the key to life.

INTRODUCTION

Please take from this book, that which is right for you at this moment in time. My aim is to share that which I have learnt. It is not to force any opinions on anyone, as my intentions are of pure love and light. If your views differ. This in no way means that your, or my views are wrong. It just means we are seeing things from a different perspective.

The first chapter is more of an introduction to the book, from where we will delve into a little more depth. We all at some point or other seem to be asking the same questions. Why are we here? How did we come into being? What happens when we leave this world?

All we can do is share that which we have learnt on our journey of life so far and hopefully, the more we all share, the more we will come to understand.

So far it's been a fascinating journey full of highs, lows and mind boggling headaches, but most definitely fun.

Read on to find out about the law of attraction and how it works. We will go into the reasons it goes wrong for some of us and give tips on how to turn it around.

We will go into more depth, showing how all different kinds of help can change the way we think and help break lifetime habits once thought impossible to break.

Further on, you will see the effects of illness and pain released through the ability to let go of unknown stress taken on in the body. I will share with you my own personal experiences, releasing enough stress to free myself from continually taking ongoing prescriptions of medication. Explanations of how the body functions in connection with its creation, as far back as the beginning of time. We will look at the connections of the law of attraction, with both religions and science. Giving an understanding as to how and why they exist and are all, so important. Connecting with our evolution, past, present and future.

If you've read this far... Read on, the time for you is NOW! The change is happening, so jump on board and enjoy the ride. It really is possible to find a better life, no matter how good you think it is right now.

Chapters

already have in your life, however big or small is a sure way to receive more. Suppose your car broke down and you have to get the bus and stand waiting in the cold. Be grateful that there is a bus and that you have a nice comfy ride and can sit back and relax, knowing you will soon arrive at your destination. The key is to always look for the positive.

Here is an example of turning a negative into a positive… My ex-husband and I owned a car wash on the A556 and it was a thriving business with a very good name, he always wanted his business in our hometown. For some reason, I decided we should expand and we got another small car wash out of town. We also expanded with a mobile side of the business. No sooner had all this been put in place, the banks started to collapse and the business felt the effects of the credit crunch. Shortly after one thing lead to another and we lost our main business, leaving us with the small car wash and mobile business to tide us over. Instead of being angry and upset at that which we had lost. We instead focused our attentions on being grateful for that which we still had, a small business to keep us going. You may not think it but all this was a positive. Had none of this happened we would still be on the A556. Because of the struggle, he pestered our next landlord for some land in our hometown. Only through his persistence were we given the opportunity to occupy, not the land we had originally asked to rent but an even better site in a better location. His dream had been to have his business in a prime spot in our hometown. Without what seemed at the time to be negative outcomes and our positivity throughout, my ex-husband's dream would not have materialised. When one door closes, another door opens.

Many of us ask for something and then just as it's about to happen we lose faith. We say something negative like "I'll never get that car" and as fast as that, the universe just received a negative and thinks oh you don't want it anymore and stops it from happening. Also our actions have to match our thoughts. It's no good thinking you're going to have that car if you're saying out loud something different also do your feelings match your thoughts. Do you feel belittled in any way as you wave to your friend whilst waiting at the bus stop, as he or she drives past in their nice new sports car. If we want to have something that makes us feel good, then we have to feel good for other people's achievements as well as our own.

So where's the scientific proof? There is proof, but it's all a question of how much proof we need. For some the proofs we have already are not enough or solid enough. Most people refuse to believe in things like phones and TVs, until they are actually there in front of us and we try them out for ourselves. The more miraculous things we come across in reality, the more open minded we become. For some, the only real proof of the law of attraction is to try it out. It doesn't always happen straight away. This may take some practice. Being negative is a behaviour pattern that has been learned over many years. These habits aren't always easily broken. Many great scientists were not believed until they could prove their findings. However look at what we have today, electricity, gas, televisions, telephones, computers, aeroplanes, cars. Technology is advancing all the time and so are we. It's a proven fact that we only use a fraction of our brains. Yet we see more and more people learning to tap into the universal energy to know things that haven't yet happened. More people are learning to use this energy to heal their bodies from dis-ease. People who do tai chi learn to feel the universal energy around them, while others just turn on the TV which is plugged into the universal energy. (Yes, good old electricity.)

So how did we come to be so negative?

Being born is a trauma in itself. Even in the womb, a developing embryo will be passed genes with traumatic memory from parents. Just as a computer stores its history. A person stores its history of its life, in its genes. Some of which will be passed on such as looks and hereditary diseases such as illnesses, fears, phobias etc. Not to mention any stress picked up from the mother's emotional state during pregnancy. We all pick up stress on a daily basis, even during the night when sleeping. I'm sure we've all experienced the fright we get when waking up from a nightmare.

From then on we go out into the big wide world to pick up more stress and learned behavioural patterns, both positive and negative. With that we develop ways to protect ourselves. These ways of protecting ourselves, aren't always in our own best interests.

For example some sulk to receive attention, which eventually causes the opposite when the other person feels they cannot help. Others may be stubborn and dig their heels in as a way of preventing others from expecting too much, this only pushes people away. People use wit and sarcasm to hide their true feelings, however they are not dealing with their true emotions. Instead, they are burying them to later in life find their release in disease. Many hide their anger to save hurting other people's feelings, this only leads to loss of control when the anger finally erupts. Sometimes we lie to protect others and ourselves, causing anxiety and frustration when people do not believe our truth. Another bad habit is to put others down as a way of putting ourselves up, this only shows our hidden insecurities and offends others causing unwelcome reactions. They are all forms of emotional blackmail which is negative energy. This will only attract a negative outcome from others and ourselves eventually.

All these and more, are habits that we have developed in order to try and protect ourselves. If you want to know what habits you have formed, look at the people in front of you. Any negative habit that you have however slight, you will find will irritate you or will certainly be noticeable in the people that surround you. From our experience as we notice and let go of old habits, either the people fall away from our company or those who we were irritated by do not irritate anymore. It's sometimes the case that we just don't notice those habits anymore.

So how should we get our point across without hurting ourselves and others? First of all you need to treat yourself with the love and respect you deserve, only then will you treat others the same way. Never feel that you deserve less than others, we are all connected as one and therefore all deserve the same respect. Rather than blaming yourself or others, step back from your emotions and dispassionately study the problem at hand. You can then come to a solution without projecting blame towards anyone. Ask yourself what is the problem, not who is the problem. You can then begin to find real solutions with productive outcomes.

You can't fix life by working on your mind alone, it needs to be balanced out by releasing physical energy. If all of your energy is concentrated in your head it will cause headaches. The body needs a physical release, which is where exercise and creativity come in. A writer needs to create a piece that can be read by others, thoughts on paper. A painter needs to take their pictures out of their thoughts and physically produce it on paper or canvas. We also need exercise, if we don't use the physical body it will loose its ability to be used. This is why it is also important for us to look after our body by eating healthily. The more nutritious the food and drink that we put into our body's, plays an important part in fueling both the mind and body for life functions. We are now beginning to realise the importance of releasing the blocked negative energy, causing harm that we have already done to ourselves. We need to open up to the understanding of many holistic therapies. These include massage which loosens the muscles by manipulation, releasing tension caused by stress which is a negative blocked energy. This can be pushed around the body to get it loosened and flowing again. Reiki works in the same way, but less physical. This time the mind of the therapist works with the higher mind of the client, to remove blocked energy and replace it with positive energy or to transmute it within the body to get it flowing again. The energy is universal energy and the clients higher mind is always in control. Tai chi is a form of relaxation, and learning to feel the energy surrounding the body. Yoga is a way of relaxing the muscles in the body, so that the energy can flow more easily. The more we use breath or breathing to relax the muscles in our body, the more subtle we become. Acupuncture is the use of needles in the same way that a masseur can find sore spots in the body, which when loosened can release pain in other areas of the body. An acupuncturist does the same thing by pin pointing those points and releasing the pressure with a needle. Meditation is a relaxation allowing the mind to rest and the higher mind to take over. This also allows the body to relax. Probably one of the most important things we can do to balance ourselves, is to have fun. Fun and laughter are a great way to release stress.

Life is supposed to be fun, not hard work and when we stop trying to force things and push against things everything actually becomes so much easier. The fact is that more often than not, it is our own fears that hold us back from making the most out of our time here on earth.

But it's not just our fault you might say. I don't have the money to go out and make the most of life. I work all the hours only to have money taken off me. Where's the fairness in that?

We seem to have got to a point in life where a few are ruling the majority, this often seems to be the case with not just ourselves but animals too. The strongest is always in charge. The unfairness seems to be when we make a stand. To stand against the strongest or most powerful, we are always going to need to pull together if we are going to win. We can't complain if we are willing to just sit and take it everything takes a little effort. We don't have to use brute force, but we can set things in motion.

In the late 80s early 90s poll tax was introduced into the U.K. It started with a few refusing to pay and as many did not agree with the poll tax, many joined in doing the same. Some people were taken to court for none payment, but because there were too many to take to court the cases were dismissed. Others who were too afraid to join in would not pay until the very last minute, when they felt they had to. I have to categorise myself in this one. Because many stood together, they became a force to be reckoned with and poll tax was abolished. The sad thing is, if we allow things to go too far and others to have too much control over us. When we finally stand up for ourselves there can be consequences. As in this case many were sent to prison for a short time, until it was realised that there just wasn't going to be enough room for the amount of people refusing to pay. So do others have the right to take our hard earned money against our wishes? No one does but the fact is we let them. We all go along with the process and we participate in handing over our hard earned cash. Let's face it, we want many of the things that are offered to us in return. Most things start with good intention. The difficulty occurs when every situation is different and what started as a great helpful idea, becomes out of balance. To stop people from pushing the boundaries, rules are put in writing. When this happens we then lose our right to use our discretion. Of course none of us are perfect and will never get it completely right controlling others, as we have a hard enough job controlling ourselves. We are like vehicles that need a service every so often, or computers that need defragmenting. Too many of us are to busy blaming someone else or something else for that which we don't have.

We need to be more assertive and stand our ground in the very beginning. It's a fact that people get greedy. It's part of our imbalanced evolution. When we watch a film we enjoy, it's hard to tare ourselves away. When we get an adrenaline rush we want more of the same. We're too scared to go on that fair ride, but we've just got to. It's what drives us to move forward. The problem is we make mistakes and our mistakes affect others as well as ourselves. Sometimes we get these feelings from doing the wrong things for the wrong reasons. We argue with people over the silliest of things because if we win the argument we feel empowered, however if we lose we feel deflated. If we learn by the mistakes we make great, but sometimes were a little slow to catch on and so keep making the same mistakes over and over again. Those in power for instance, may have started with all good intentions. But somewhere along the line they got hooked on the need for more power and being in control. So they forgot the key importance of acting out of love for everyone as a whole and instead starting to focus on themselves or on the bigger picture, not thinking of those they trample on in the process. This is where we all find difficulties in getting the balance right for both ourselves and others. We can start by wanting the best for others, yet if we leave ourselves out of the equation we find that others will push beyond our boundaries wanting to take too much from us. When this happens we leave ourselves deflated or with too little in life, until we learn by sometimes getting angry and taking back for ourselves. The problem is, if we allow too much of this to go on. We then tip the scales too far in the opposite direction and become selfish by keeping too much for ourselves, for fear of others taking from us. If we don't learn that we are missing something out the lessons will keep coming until eventually something big will happen to force us back in line with the flow of life. The more powerful the person and the more people involved, whether knowingly connected in some way or not. The bigger the disaster.

Take the recent recession for instance. Those who got too greedy for power and money at the top, triggered a disaster that affected people worldwide. The fact is that we all play a part in allowing others to be in control of us. We may not want to fight back because we know we won't like the immediate consequences. But when a disaster happens, everyone starts to pull together. Yes there will always be those who won't and they will go on to learn the hard way yet again. Those who start to focus on others around them as well as looking after themselves will pull through, if they get the balance right.

What about natural disasters? We may not cause them, yet they play an important part in our teachings. When disaster strikes we suddenly stop thinking of what we are allowed to do by law, or under the health and safety rules (All rules that we have imposed upon ourselves). We suddenly do the right thing for all concerned. We think about others as well as ourselves. We all pull together putting ourselves at risk to help those in need. We come together like a family, as one.

Those who are born into poverty, have lessons to learn just like the rest of us. The problem we have in poverty, is we see the lack of everything before us. When we see this day in day out, that is what our minds are focused on. While we focus on scarcity, that is exactly what we are creating more of. There are always a few who can break free from poverty. These are possibly some of the dreamers. The one thing that these people have different to others, is that they believe. They don't allow others to sway their belief in themselves and they act on their impulse taking the necessary steps to get them where they want to be. It always seems easier for us to focus on that which we don't have, than that which we could have. This is because we find it hard to let go of that which hurts or upsets us.

One of my daughters Jade, was a great example of drawing to her what she wanted. There was an Easter competition held each year at school. She bought a ticket like everyone else. The difference with my daughter, was that she had decided that that egg was hers and she was going to win it. In her eyes it already belonged to her. Sure enough she came home with the egg. My eldest daughter Chelsey cottoned on and during her last year at that school, she too came home with her class Easter egg. Each year following. Jade won the class egg. The last year she attended primary school, she told me there was an Easter egg competition for the whole school as well as the one for the class. Leading up to the competitions everyone was saying how Jade would win and there was little point them entering. I said to my daughter, "You've won every year because you believed you could, now everyone believes the same. You can't lose" That year she came home with both eggs. She is one of those people with a strong wilful mind and I don't doubt that once she has decided what she wants, she will always land on her feet so to speak.

We are all one, so a child born into poverty is suffering the effects of a bigger part of us. We are all connected due to the fact that we are all from the same source. This is how we affect each other. We can't always see it physically, but we are interconnected on a level of vibration that cannot be seen by the naked eye. However we can feel the effects of our interconnection, especially at such times like when we argue. This triggers emotions and feelings in our bodies. Some children may carry on in the same everyday way of life, however others will learn more and faster and move forward one way or another. The fact is that a child born in poverty is not necessarily poorer than a child born into riches. There are different kind of riches and prosperity. They don't have to be materialistic. God is the good inside every single one of us, we are all one in the same. Scientists have proven that we are in fact created from energy and energy creates everything else. As energy cools down it turns into matter i.e. dust. From there it evolves into all that we see today. So when religions teach us that we are made from the dust of the earth, that is exactly so.

According to scientists, all matter exists with a force that connects us all. Religions use God as our creator and connection. If we are all connected to god then we are all connected to each other.

So why do we have different religions? The law of attraction is religious teachings just interpreted differently. Because the same deep down belief system has developed in different parts of the world and passed down over time.

So if they are the same belief system, why do they all contradict each other? Or do they? First of all, man on earth wrote these teachings and re-wrote them over time. As we have come to realise down here on earth, we all have free will and constantly make mistakes as a way of learning. We also find that the bible contradicts itself for example, one part will say 'an eye for an eye' where another part will say 'turn the other cheek'. Many of us will read this thinking they are mistakes, but are they? In all cases to win an argument the easiest solution is to walk away, therefore turning the other cheek. There are times when we cannot walk away from a situation as it may follow us until we turn around, face it head on and stand up for ourselves. Therefore 'an eye for an eye'. In saying this we can understand that we only do as much as we need to do to defend ourselves and no more. We see things differently from different perspectives and from our own knowing. They are in fact all right from their own perspective. As time goes on, language and the way we speak changes which is why more recent versions are more understandable than older versions. This is because they have been written from a new perspective as we evolve. Strip every religion back to its main belief system and every religion believes in something that is greater than ourselves which is of pure love. The different teachings are there to teach us how we came to be and how to get the most out of life. It teaches our purpose in life, which is to be pure love ourselves. As we try to teach our children to be good, which we do not always get it right and we make mistakes along the way. So do the people who teach that which has been written or passed down in the teachings. This is because we all see things from our own knowing and possibly different perspectives.

We all too often make the mistake of thinking abundance is money, power and materialistic things. However true abundance is quality of life which is pure happiness, which only comes from love. This is what all the teachings teach us to strive for.

So how do scientists explain our being here?

The law of gravity i.e. The law of attraction.

All matter originates and exists by virtue of a force that connects all. Interpreted... we are here by the grace of god. Therefore we all exist by the connection of a loving force. Quantum physicists have now stumbled on what mystics have been saying for over thousands of years. That reality is a projection of the mind. They have found that reality does not exist without the mind defining it, therefore it is our mind which creates our reality. Meaning everything that exists before us cannot come into fruition, until we have conjured it up in our mind first. We are all evolving and finding the truth as to how and why we are here. We are all on the same journey just different paths.

THE LAW OF ATTRACTION

What is the law of attraction?

The law of attraction is known as a few different things. Religions call it God, the all mighty power that governs the earth. He may go by different names in different religions, but never the less we are all talking about the same thing.

It's also known as the law of gravity or the law of nature. These all have the same description, the all mighty power that governs the earth. Whatever we believe, we are in fact heading in the same direction. You see God teaches love of all things. He teaches that if we do wrong we will be punished. The law of attraction shows that what we give out comes back to us. So if you're thinking or giving out harm to others, it will in fact always return to the source of where it came from in the first place Teaching us a valuable lesson, as we don't like harm to ourselves. It teaches us to be good. Of course, all the good thoughts we project, also have to come back to us.

So why all the arguments over who's right and who's wrong?

For some it all comes down to fear. We get in a comfort zone of what we believe to be and when someone tells us differently, we become afraid of losing that which gave us comfort. The fact is, that to see someone else's point of view and even to accept it. We don't have to lose that which we already knew. When we are taught from all different perspectives such as religions, philosophers and scientists, physicists and astronomers. We actually gain a greater understanding as everything seems to complement everything else.

We have all come from god our father in heaven and so we have all come from that very first spark of energy that created the Big Bang. So we are all agreed that we are all connected. Just like a mother knows when her young ones need her and siblings connect with each other. Just because we separated into separate pieces of matter, doesn't mean that we are not still a part of each other.

My children will always be a part of me and always connected by my thoughts and love for them. My close friend who lives half way round the world, always thinks about me on the days leading up to my emails to her and vice versa.

We don't have to lose the myths and legends. We don't have to replace our bibles, for they are all based on the truth. Some just need their truth to be more solid and proven in a way that they can understand. So it all seems simple enough, think good thoughts and only good will come back to us.

Why do we have such complications?

Maybe we don't actually realise what we are doing until it's too late. By the time we realise the first ever mistake we made, it has had such a knock on effect that one thing has built up on top of the other. This happens until our reactions have become habits, that even if we notice them they will be hard to shift.

Where are we going wrong?

Ever wonder why things aren't going your way, and life just isn't fare sometimes? You look around you and some people always seem to be upbeat and happy. While others are moody, miserable and feel hard done by. So I presume because you are reading this book you are looking for the key to life, just as I was.

First of all you need to understand that like attracts like. So a person who wakes up one morning feeling miserable with low self-esteem, is going to spend the rest of the day attracting more of the same. Leaving you feeling even worse than you did when you woke up. In the same way if you wake up one morning feeling happy, because the sun is out and the birds are singing making you feel good. You carry on through the day meeting happy people with a brighter outlook and everything seemingly going your way Yes there are always exceptions.

Supposing you driving to work happy, upbeat and ready for the day ahead. You suddenly hear a beep aimed at you, from an irate driver. All because you just forgot to indicate, or sat a little too long at the traffic lights. You have a choice. You either take it on board and allow it to make you feel upset or angry. Which will then change your mood and that which you attract for the rest of the day. Or you can just smile, apologise and accept that they may be having a bad day or are not feeling very patient today. You can then carry on through the day feeling happy and attracting happy people, with everything running smoothly. Not everyone feels the same at the same time and no one feels the same all of the time. So you are going to come across people of a different frequency or mood to yourself. It is up to you whether you allow them to affect you or not. Ultimately you are in control of your own emotions, even though it doesn't always feel like it. We just need to learn how to control them, have a little determination as old habits are going to have to be broken and healing of the mind and body will need to occur.

Ok so that it sounds easy enough, but if it were that simple we would be able to change over night. We have all been putting negative thoughts and emotions out into the universe for many years, as well as positive. These all go out on different frequency levels, attracting that which is of the same frequency. Therefore picking up more of the same and eventually always returning to source i.e. Back to ourselves. Here is where we get the old saying.. 'What you give out in life, comes back to you three fold.' So if you have a great day and something goes wrong, you may be receiving a little of what you have already given out before that day.

I found, whist trying to change. By being happy and positive and believing that everything is good. It would last for a spell and then things would go wrong and I would feel low again. I would then have to pick myself up. Tell myself that everything was good and that everything was going right to change my life back onto a good frequency. For those few days, while I'd felt low. I came to realise that I had already sent it out into the universe and it had to come back to me. The more I practiced picking myself up, the longer the happy spells lasted.

CONTENTMENT

So we want more out of life. We won't be content at the top until we learn to be content where we are now. That doesn't mean we can't have more out of life, it just means we have to appreciate what we have now. If we can't appreciate what we have now, then the universe has nothing left to give us. This is because everything that comes no matter how great, will feel just as it does now. If you don't notice the great things in your life now, you won't notice them in your future.

I'm not only grateful for the wonderful positive things in my life. I have learned to accept and show gratitude for those down days in my life. You see without these temporary unhappy times in my life I may not have the drive to push myself on for better things. Without those bad days, I may have been too comfortable to push forward and fulfill my dreams. However big or small my dreams be, it's sometimes too easy to do nothing and procrastinate.

We now see how important it is to be grateful. If we are ungrateful, we might as well be moaning out loud about all the things we are ungrateful for. We now know that, that will go out into the universe attracting more of the same. As the universe does not distinguish between good and bad, it just delivers. Here on earth it is our free will to choose what we want in our lives. If we can actually find something good from a bad situation, then any bad that comes our way will only teach us something good. We sometimes have to experience that which we don't want in order to know that which we do want.

Another way we fail to use the law of attraction correctly, is when our actions and thoughts aren't in line with each other.

Believing alone that you can change something in your life, won't work without the actions to match the thoughts. The brain is connected to your thoughts and the feelings in your body. If the thoughts are telling your brain one thing and your bodily actions are that of something different. For instance if your thoughts are telling your brain that your body is fit and healthy, yet your body is being fed with junk and getting no exercise. Then the brain is getting mixed messages. In the same way doing everything in your power to make your body healthy, look and feel good. Yet constantly telling yourself the opposite. Then no matter what you do, you will never feel good about yourself.

I have noticed this in my daughters as they have grown up. When they eat healthy, go to the gym and want to feel good about themselves. They will constantly focus on a part of their body that has a certain amount of fat or muscle on it. Such as the thighs, which need a certain amount to support the body. They will focus on this part of their body and no matter how slim they get, they cannot see it. My point being they have forgotten to focus on the positive aspects being the beautiful slim, shapely figure as a whole.

For another example of thoughts not matching actions.

Suppose you have taken and passed all the exams needed to qualify you to get that job you have pinned your hopes on. You make the phone call, fill in the application form and go for the interview. You have done everything it takes to get the job you want, but deep down you are worried.

You tell yourself you haven't done enough and that you won't get the job. This is a prime example of your thoughts not being in line with your actions. If your worries (thoughts and feelings) are so strong that they start to affect your actions i.e. your posture drops, your voice isn't convincing. Then your thoughts have become stronger than your actions and there is more chance of being unsuccessful than successful.

We can want all the wonderful things in the world we can focus on them, believe in them and do our most to attract them. If we are not in a good place ourselves i.e. we don't truly love and appreciate ourselves all our sins and mistakes in life. Then we are not truly feeling good about ourselves. Yes, some of these things can still come to us, but they will not be without their flaws. We can only draw to us that which is of the same frequency.

Our energy vibrates. The happier we are, the lighter we feel because we vibrate at a high frequency.

The lower we feel the slower our energy vibrates making us feel less energetic.

Notice people who bounce from one relationship to another. The process reoccurs unless we give ourselves time to grieve the loss of one relationship and the time and ability to pick ourselves upto a point where we feel good about ourselves and others. We can only attract those of same frequency.

So if you are looking for a happy go lucky partner who will give you all your heart's desire. If you're still feeling low before you meet them, you can bet your life they have some deep issue waiting to rise up and burst your bubble.

One of the worst things we do, is losing patience. Down here on earth, we only have a lifetime. So we want everything to happen NOW, or as soon as possible. A child hasn't yet learnt that there are obstacles stopping them from getting what they want. So their belief is a lot stronger, as they believe they can have things straight away. They do not yet understand the need of waiting for things and are much more likely to receive what they want. As an adult, we have lived and learned in a society of both negative and positive aspects. We are brought up with sayings such as... 'You don't get anything for nothing.' Telling us that we have to work hard to get anything we want in life.

I was brought up with the saying 'money doesn't grow on trees' and 'you don't get anything for nothing in this world'. 'No money, no honey' is another.

They are all reiterating that money is hard to come by. That we have to struggle to get what we want in life and that things don't come easy. Planting a negative seed in our minds. Because down here on earth time is so important to us, we lose faith when things don't happen straight away. Or we lose patience when things don't happen fast enough. We start to listen to those little seeds that were planted with old sayings. Causing us to lose faith and disbelieve that which we had once believed in, or once convinced ourselves that it was going to come true. The minute this happens we cancel out that which we expected in the first place, as the universe thinks we no longer want it to happen. We also need to stay positive when things seem to go wrong as sometimes things have to fall away to make way for the new.

Our faith in things to happen is not always strong enough to give us the belief, that it is actually going to happen when we desire it. In other words we do not act in the now. If we dream about things in the future without setting a time limit, or acting as though we already have the reality. The dream will stay in the future, which is exactly where we believe it to be. In the same way if we constantly think about, upsetting or tragic events and experiences from the past. Succumbing to our emotions that we felt and possibly still feel. We are keeping it in the now which like a dream, or goal will cause it to reappear in our future and present.

Ever wondered what happens when we watch a scary movie, or a drama that has us in tears and gets our emotions flowing. If reality goes out into the universe, what happens when we totally lose ourselves in T.V. or other aspects such as radio, books, computer games etc. When our senses pick up the emotions of these things, such as fear and sadness. Our brain does not distinguish between reality and make believe, as in reality nothing is impossible. Therefore our body will take on stress, from these things just as it does in normal everyday living So what we take in, we are also putting out into the universe. Which is why the more problems we see on T.V. etc. more of the same actually goes on in life. The same happens when we watch the news. Have you ever noticed how it's nearly all bad news? The more we see and hear, the more we worry and stress bringing it into our everyday lives. Take cancer for example. It's constantly on the T.V. adverts, magazines etc. It doesn't matter if it's about the cancer itself or a cure for it, the fact is it's being focused on. I've come across more people lately with cancer than any other illness or disease. Yet before all this came to light and before all this focus on finding a cure. I hadn't come across one. If we want to raise funds we should put the focus on good health or something positive then fund those who are actually focusing on the cure itself. This way it keeps our focus on incurable diseases to a minimum.

How do we get it right?

First of all, we need to clear out the clutter. All these negative habits and negative thinking, must go. Ha-ha it's not that simple. So here's a few tips to help. Start by lifting your mood, remember you are the one who controls your emotions. So put on some happy music, hum a cheerful tune, take yourself for a walk. Nature is great for uplifting the spirit. Go and have some fun, do whatever it is that makes you feel happy. Make right now feel good and be grateful for it. You have now put yourself on the right frequency to attract more of the same. Now the hard part is staying on the right frequency. Enjoy it for as long as it lasts, but learn to become aware of when it slips. So you bump into someone who is not on the same frequency as you, who certainly doesn't appreciate that you feel great while they feel miserable. So they may want to sap a little of your energy, in order to pick themselves up a little. Look for your choices. Can you walk away from this? If not accept the way they feel and understand that it is their problem to deal with and not your problem to take on. This doesn't mean that we can't listen to people and help them as we go through life. It just means that you learn to stay on your own happy vibration, allowing them to join you or to stay where they are. Do not allow yourself to join them. If this happens pull yourself away.

We often find ourselves in situations where we feel helpless or that things are out of our control. Everything we do to combat this is about finding the right balance. It helps to try and see the other persons point of view and try to understand why they behave the way they do. Some people will constantly grind us down with their life story full of problems. It gives them a little lift if someone else is showing an interest in them. If we fail to give them the attention they're looking for they will find another way to stay hooked on the drama. Possibly causing arguments. If they can make someone feel lower than themselves it makes them feel a little better. Let's face it even If we don't like constant drama in our lives we can still get hooked on it, without even realising when it comes around. What we need to realise is that however much drama we have in our lives. If it is not positive it will never satisfy us. If we are constantly looking for attention, no matter how we go about it. Whether we lie and make up stories or belittle people to get a reaction. We will never quench the inadequate feeling until we find the root cause. No matter how much we listen or how much attention we give to someone with this feeling. It will never be enough. Not everyone wants real help and not everyone is ready to be helped. We have to step back and allow each other to learn and progress at a rate that is right for each individual. Every situation is different and it's sometimes trial and error to find something that works. The key is to do whatever it is you do out of loving kindness for everyone concerned, including yourself. Now here's another tip... Whatever you do you need to focus on what you want, and again this needs to be something or someone who is positive. The last thing we want to do is focus on all the stuff we just had in our lives that we don't want, creating and attracting more of the same. The key is to get the balance right. There are going to be times when we should help, times when we should walk away and times when we should stand up for ourselves. If what you do is out of loving kindness for everyone, you won't go wrong. This is because that loving kindness that you are giving out, is always going to return to source i.e. YOU.

The next key factor in the law of attraction. Gratitude. We now have to find something in this situation to be grateful for. In order to help us find that, we can look at the situation deciding exactly which parts we would like to keep and which parts we would like to lose. Supposing you are in a job. Is it a job you love and would like to stay in, in which case there is the first thing for you to be grateful for. Or is it a job that you would quite happily leave for something better given the opportunity? If so it's time to focus on the job you would really like to have. From there you can start to look for anything surrounding this situation, that you would like to keep in your life. Such as focusing on those you work with and get on well with. Or new people that you would like to work with and the types of personalities that you would like to surround yourself with. It may just be the money aspect, in which case you are grateful because you are in a well paid job. Or you focus your attentions on the amount of money you would like to earn. If nothing else be grateful for being shown that which you don't want, to help give you a better idea of that which you do. As hard as it may seem, there is always something to be grateful for.

Now align your actions with your thoughts. Supposing the job you're in, isn't right for you and you decide you want a better one. You must still do this job to the best of your ability knowing that in your next job you will be just as good at it, if not better. The universe needs to know that you want something enough to want to do it well. If you go through life half heartedly, the universe doesn't know if you really want it or not. In the same way if you keep worrying about those people that drain you, while focusing on the people you would like to have around you. You are sending out mixed messages. Only when you make a strong conviction in your decisions, can the universe act. When you have made your decision, you must believe and accept that it is being dealt with and will happen. Not only that, you must start to take the necessary steps. Doors will start to open and as you say yes to these opportunities, more of them will come. If you ignore them or walk away from them, your sending the message that you don't want it anymore and the opportunities will fizzle out.

Our faith in things to happen, has to be strong enough to believe that it is actually going to happen when we desire. In which case we have to start preparing for it. So if you want a new house, you have to start looking around for the house you want. Start clearing out the clutter and preparing ready for the big upheaval of moving house. You may look deeper into which removal firm you will use when the time comes. All this helps you believe more and more that this is actually going to happen. When it does you will be ready. This is a way of bringing the future into the now. Another way to do this is to believe you have something right now. So if you want a new car. Go out and sit in that new car, take it for a test drive and feel how it would actually feel to own it. Feel all the emotions and the excitement that you will feel when you pick up the keys and drive it home for the first time. See yourself parking it in your drive. Keep this feeling going by writing it down and re-reading it, by putting up a picture where you will see it constantly or by talking as though you already own it. Don't lose faith or start to waiver, because it seems to be taking forever. Where is it in your mind? If it's in the future, it's probably going to stay there. So bring it into the now, or put a realistic time on it that you can believe. You have to believe without a shadow of a doubt that things will be as you want them by a specific time, or believe that they are right now. If it doesn't happen on time or straight away, believe that something better is in its place. When something falls through, it is because something even better is just around the corner. When one door closes, another door opens. There are many old sayings that have developed from truth. Too many of us wait until it's just around the corner, so close and yet we suddenly stop believing. Don't undo the good that you have created. Remember, you only want the good stuff in the now and your future. So don't focus on bad things that have already happened and don't give your attention to bad things that are currently occurring.

My youngest daughter was bullied in her first year of high school, to the point of having to leave. Seeing what she went through broke my heart. The pain was so bad and we were so hurt and angry that we found it hard to let go, we both re-lived the emotions over and over daily. This caused the bully to reappear in our lives constantly in one way or another, which made it even harder to move forward. We had moved away from the problem but because our emotions didn't match our actions the problem came with us. If we didn't see the bully someone would be talking about her. As we couldn't get her out of our minds, the only other way to deal with this was to try and forgive. In order to do this I had to see her as any other person with her own problems and detach from the personal vendetta. The feelings of forgiveness didn't come straight away but never the less, I kept on telling myself the positive and slowly over time the pain lessened. Eventually, she stopped appearing at the same places or she just wasn't noticed with the same powerful presence of being center of attention, but instead faded into the background and was heard of less and less. Knowing the law of attraction helped us through this situation faster and easier than if we had not known and understood it. Teachers were amazed at how quickly my daughter had gone from being so afraid to confidently being on stage, making friends and constantly smiling.

No matter how bad things get, we have the power to change them for the better. Look for what you want and you will find it. If you firmly make the decision to get what you want out of life, the doors will surely open and as long as you walk through the doors of opportunity. You really can't fail. It's not hard work to do something that excites you. When we want something, we want to do the necessary to get it. Go with the flow because getting what we want is a part of life and doing the work to get it is the fun part. Life is supposed to be fun so do what you enjoy to get what makes you happy, you deserve it!

We have now learnt how to bring the past into the future and the now. Here is how we bring the future into the present. We all daydream, but how many of our dreams actually come into reality? Dreaming about our future alone just keeps it in the future. Using the things that we have already learnt, helps to bring us that which we desire. In order to fetch the future into the now, we need to see it as though it has already come into being. Firstly setting realistically achievable goals as stepping stones, helps us to believe the dreams can be achieved. It's like breaking everything down into baby steps, we can strengthen these steps by setting a date that we can conceive as a realistic time for this goal to be achieved. We can always change things as we go along, keeping our thoughts and actions in line with each other. If everything is in place and everything is right for our highest will and good doors will start to open. It is important that when setting goals, you are ready to take the necessary steps through the open doors. We can all dream of becoming rich and famous should someone offer you to talk or perform in front of people, (which would be a necessary step to where you want to be). Would you be ready and have the confidence to do this? All too often the fear factor kicks in and we become too afraid to take the necessary steps. This is because we are setting the goals too high. When we refuse to walk through the open door, we tell the universe that we don't want it anymore and would prefer to stay in our comfort zone.

It's like learning to swim. As a child if we jumped into a big pool of water having never had the experience, our immediate reaction would be that of panic. Because we haven't gone through the stepping stones of learning to swim and feeling comfortable in water.

When I first took my children to a pool, their immediate reaction was to stay out of the water. After having watched me get in and having a little encouragement, they were then ready for the first step of putting their hands and feet in to feel the water. In time they were ready for the next step, of perhaps sitting on a step slightly below water level. Once they had got used to the water flowing around their legs, they would go in a step deeper feeling the water around their body. They would take each step little by little until they had learnt and built up the confidence to be able to comfortably get in the pool where they could learn to swim. Fear was there to protect them and it was never necessary to push out of the comfort zone past the fear barrier. Every step could still be taken to achieve the desired outcome. On progressing, the adrenaline of achieving something would always drive my children further.

The point being, set your goals realistically and small enough for you to achieve. Be as kind to yourself as you would a child.

On the other hand, we can walk through the doors as they open. Find that more and more doors keep opening and opportunities keep coming our way. We are now bringing our dreams closer and closer into reality.

Learn to listen to and feel the emotions within your body.

Our natural state is in the flow of life. Our emotions are designed to help us stay there. When we stop listening to our bodies' rhythm, we stop noticing when it is trying to tell us something. This is why yoga, tai chi, prayer and other forms of meditation are important. They help us listen to our bodies' rhythm. Excitement is a rush of adrenalin that keeps us moving forward and wanting to experience new things. It goes wrong when we get hooked on wanting too many materialistic things instead of quality of life. We need the two to be balanced in order to experience true abundance. There is a need to take control when we feel fear. Fear is there as a message to protect us and keep us within the flow of life. When we push forward too fast, we are pushing against the flow causing mishaps in order to slow us down. Which is why things go wrong and accidents happen. When we need to take control, we can get hooked on the adrenalin rush wanting more until we feel the need for power. We all know what happens when people are out of flow with too much power. On the other hand there are those of us who get trapped in fear and become stuck, staying with only that which they already know. The more you get hooked on something, the harder it is to let go. We can now see why it is so important not to feed people who are hooked on power with more negative ideas. They will play it over and over in their minds until it comes into being. The more things people do to get an adrenalin rush the more they need to do to keep it going. If the rush is coming from something good that's great. If it comes from doing something bad, it's only going to get worse. This is why it is so important to concentrate on positive, good things in life and not the negative bad things. We need more positive uplifting programs and films on T.V. We need to see the wonderful truths (the things that go right in the world) on the news and in the papers. We need more positive books out there to read. There are great things that go on in life that we love to hear about. So why keep looking for all the bad stuff. It starts with each and every one of us. If we show less Interest in negative things and more interest in positive. Those who supply the products will change what they provide for us. We can already see a shift in films as they are slowly starting to show the law of attraction in their stories. We need to see more and more positive aspects in absolutely everything.

THE PITFALLS

Perfection is love.

Perfection can only be achieved with positivity (love) as it pulls us together as one.

Perfection cannot be achieved from negativity as negativity (hate) has the opposite effect and pushes us apart.

Relationships are probably one of the hardest lessons in life. We all dream of the happy ever after, but how many of us ever really achieve it. We spend half our time seeing the other person's faults and the rest of the time trying to change them. So how is it that it's so easy to see the fault in others, yet so hard to see our own? Because deep down we all want to be perfect (i.e. we all want love). Even if we don't know it yet, it is the core of our being. When we all love each other completely it brings us all closer together, back to being one. In our relationships are lessons to help us learn unconditional love, to see our own faults would be to criticise ourselves. Which would bring emotions to the surface, that we have developed from not having unconditional love whether that be from another or from ourselves it would feel like we'd be admitting failure, in that which our inner being strives for (becoming whole again).

Where do we go wrong?

Very often when looking for a partner we seem to go for and attract those similar to our parents. A male seems to attract those who are similar to the mother and females seem to go for those similar to the father. Or they will go for the complete opposite in character. This all depends on how they were treated by their parents. For example, if we lack attention from our parents. We either go into the same relationships, keeping everyone at arm's length for fear of getting hurt or we go for the complete opposite, to gain that which we feel we have not had in our lives. Usually ending up smothered, unless we learn to balance the emotions. In a similar way, men may seek the attentions of a motherly figure that will love and care for them. However once they have this, they push it away. Often running to the pub or keeping busy to escape the attentions. Constantly complaining that they are being nagged. On the other scale they can become totally besotted or possessive and controlling. As women, we seek a father figure who will protect us and take care of us. However most men have been taught by society, that it is not right for men to show their emotions and feelings. Therefore we women go looking for that which we have missed, as well as the hardened man who will keep us safe. We then go into a relationship wanting and expecting too much. Or we get a very attentive relationship and end up feeling smothered. Seeing how we treat ourselves in conforming to society's expectations, of how we should or shouldn't behave. Puts our male and female energies out of balance. In order to have the perfect relationship both partners need to be perfectly balanced. We all too often make the mistake of replacing love with intimate relations thinking that this affection will make us feel loved and complete, as when we go into a relationship with a partner we are looking for someone to complete us. What we fail to realise is that no one else can complete us. We can only complete ourselves. This comes from unconditional pure love for our self. When we love ourselves unconditionally without judgement, with acceptance of all our faults. Only then can others treat us in the same way. This can only happen when we have learnt to and healed ourselves in order to break down every barrier that we have ever put up to protect ourselves. The barriers are habits that we have developed from birth to try and protect ourselves and others. We are always told not to upset a woman during pregnancy, because it will affect the baby or growing embryo. Birth itself is a big trauma in a person's life and has a great effect. A mother and baby are one until the baby is born. If something goes wrong at birth it can cause a hormonal in balance that affects the separation. A baby that is rejected by the mother at birth will straight away develop some way of protecting itself. To replace the love lost at birth, it may replace it with attention and cry constantly for one thing or another. Once you've developed the first habit. That then causes a reaction from others around you. On the receiving the emotional habits of others, we develop more habits of protection causing a downward spiral as we go through life. We can now see why life seems to get harder as we get older. It takes all these barriers time to build up big enough for us to see them. We first see them in others before we can see them in ourselves, because other people act like mirrors for us.

As everyone has different experiences in life, so they go on to put up different defence mechanisms. This results in different emotional states. This is why we find some people are more jealous than others. Some are quick to anger, while others shy away. Some feel the need to brag and boast, others get upset easily. There are many different emotional states and they all have a knock on effect, causing ourselves and others to put up more barriers.

As children we developed that which we've learnt from home, when we are put in an environment with other children. Nursery school and out of school clubs. A child is very vulnerable and open to learning. Lessons may be small at such an early age but are definitely continuous. A child's brain is like a new computer ready to absorb everything you put into it. There is a lot to take in and a lot of lessons to be learned. We become like a set of scales tipping this way then that, as we have emotional reactions. We then learn from our mistakes, then have more emotional reactions.

Is it any wonder by the time we get to being a teenager, some of us are ready to tip the scales too far. By now we've taken on that much stress we're totally out of balance. As our hormone levels change, we end up all over the place. Relationships are hard enough without the added anxiety of falling in love with someone. Every emotion is now emphasised and a molehill becomes a mountain. We are at a stage of development where we test boundaries in order to stand on our own two feet in the world. We rebel against any parental figure that tries to control us. This is because we have the right to free will and no one has the right to take that away from us, plenty parents would disagree with this which is why every action causes a reaction. No one wants to stand back and allow us to harm ourselves and others in the process, so they try to intervene. We cause that reaction with our own behaviour. So, we're still not learning from our mistakes. Not to worry if you are female we've got big fluctuations until we hit the menopause. Plenty of time to learn. If you are male you are maybe less fluctuating but let's face it. You do have to live alongside us women.

What it comes down to is this… The only way to get our life back to track is to stop finding fault in others. They are only reflecting back to us, our own faults. Bit harsh, but maybe we all need a wakeup call. May be our lives will change for the better because of it. It doesn't matter how small our own faults are and chances are they're not that big. The fact is that like attracts like and the lessons in front of us get bigger until we notice them. Carry on ignoring the lesson and they get bigger still. When we finally get the message and stop what we're doing. The lesson in front of us disappears.

Ever noticed people who tell lies or twist your words, so that which has been said has been turned into meaning something completely different. It may be that you do the same to others, or it could just be that you do it to yourself. There are a times when we don't like what we hear. Especially when we're young and being told we've done wrong. Or even as adults it's hard to hear a criticism. We sometimes cope by telling ourselves it wasn't our fault, or make excuses to ourselves for ourselves to help us feel a bit better about it. We may just change things ever so slightly, so things are more acceptable to us.

Don't dismiss what you see in others around you. You may have to look hard but you will find the answer somewhere, as to why you keep noticing these faults in people. When you do find it and change that habit, eventually you won't notice these things happening in others. Understanding ourselves is one of the most difficult things for us to do. So using others around you as a mirror makes it a little easier. This is because it is easier to see what's really going on when you are not emotionally involved.

Ever noticed people who come out of one bad relationship, fall back in with another just the same. This is because they haven't changed themselves. They are still attracting and are drawn to the same things in a person. We push and pull just like magnets, attracting the positives in ourselves and then fighting the negatives within ourselves. This is how people are sometimes magnetised to people they really don't get on with. Because like attracts like and if you focus on the negative aspects of a relationship, that's exactly what you're going to attract. Let's face it, if we move on from a relationship. It can sometimes leave us scarred so that we remember the hurt and pain caused, rather than remembering all that was good about the relationship.

There are other things swayed by this magnetic force and these are our mood swings. The moon has a great effect on these. It sends out frequencies and like a magnet has both positive and negative. These affect our own frequencies causing fluctuations in our moods. The moon also affects our sleep patterns due to what scientist think is our inner body clock. The problem these days is that we are not following our inner body clock.

Most of us with jobs have to be at work for a certain time and work till finishing time no matter how we feel. Children have to go to school. We cannot surrender to the flow of life i.e. working when we feel the need to work, resting when we feel the need to rest and as for fun. Well most of us just don't have enough, leaving us all totally out of balance. This leads to stress and stress leads to the need for release. We are like boiling kettles taking on more and more stress, releasing little steam in the form of illness (e.g. colds and viruses) and emotions (e.g. arguments, anger and tears). Until eventually there's so much steam that we flip our lid. Illnesses become more serious slowing us right down and making us rest when we haven't. Compressed anger erupts into someone doing something more than a heated discussion. It can become uncontrollable to the point of grievous bodily harm, or the extreme of man slaughter or murder. No wonder the world is in such a state at times.

So you think the moons a big enough challenge, wait till you hear about all the planets you have to contend with. Yes they too have frequencies affecting ours. Here's the tip of the iceberg....

As planets travel through the sky they have a different pulling power according to their position and size just like a magnet would if you were to move it around the surrounding area of metal. Or if you were to hold the nozzle of a vacuum at different positions around dust particles. When a fan or propeller spins at speed it causes suction. Planets work in a similar way. Spinning as they travel causing a pulling force just like a magnet or vacuum. Travelling mainly in the same direction as the sun according to how we see them in relation to the stars. This is known as (prograde) a Latin term meaning forward. These planets have their own cycle and at times appear to stop and reverse. The term used for this is the Latin word retrograde meaning (backward). Looking at the planets from our perspective here on earth, the planets seem to rotate forward (prograde). For a brief period they will slow down and appear to stop before spinning backwards (retrograde). In this state the planets now seem to reverse our state of being Causing problems and challenges. What can happen is this. As planets closer to earth pass by, they pass the planets further in the distance. From our position it looks like the planet in the line of vision is moving backwards. When this happens it interferes with the gravity in-between, changing its effect on us. Many think that the planets are probably too far away to affect us. This isn't true as their sheer mass and the fact that they are made up of minerals that we also contain in our bodies, is the reason they have such an effect on us.

Each of us have a planet that rules more strongly over our zodiac sign, due to its position at the time we are born into this world taking our first breath. We all have the energies from all of the planets in our solar system. We just express their different energies in different parts of our personalities. This is why we are all individual. Yet if we learn to use the planets to our advantage, balancing their energies within ourselves. We activate the power of the whole universe within us.

The energy that we take on during our first breath at birth, is the energy that starts programming our personalities. This energy is affected by many things from the push and pull of the planets with their different mineral contents, to the temperature of the energy contained in the air. In a hot humid atmosphere, the particles or atoms will move quickly and spread out. We see the effects of this as we watch steam rise from a boiling kettle. In a very cold atmosphere the particles become more still as the atmosphere becomes more solid. These atoms will then behave in a similar fashion once contained in the body programming our personalities. Of course we then have the similarities passed on from our parents and so on.

With the advances of science and astronomy we have known for a long time about the 7 main planets in our solar system. Alongside this with our advances in spirituality, we have known about the 7 main chakras of energy processing information in our bodies. As we progress, we learn and open up to more planets that exist. We also open up to the realisation that our bodies contain more chakras than the main 7 we knew to exist. We now have more main planets with others coming to light. As we realise this we are open to the possibilities of finding many more smaller planets, that we once could not see or that once did not exist. Within the body we are following the same pattern of awareness, as we find more main chakras and many more smaller chakras all over the body. Earth of course is the matter that we are made from. The planets are earth's solar system and the chakras are our solar system.

The planets rule over the zodiac signs. They have become known to us as our gods. All the zodiac signs are related to people and every person has every single planet through their birth chart, no matter how close too or far away they may be. We are all made up of the same elements contained in the planets and also the stars. Therefore every person with the ability to balance the whole of the universes energy within them, becomes the god of themselves. This is because in a balanced state, our brains are able to access and process the information contained in the universe more clearly through our bodies.

Understanding the planets will lead us to understanding the human body. Understanding the human body will help us to understand the planets. They are part of us and we are part of them!

We are a part of the whole universe crammed into bodies, recreating life as we know it

The universe creates, we create.

The universe is an Intelligence, we are an intelligence.

The universe is still expanding, we are still evolving.

Every element has an opposite, every person is a mirror of ourselves.

Therefore the law of attraction can only bring to us that which we think feel, visualise and do.

The law of attraction will bring to us in our everyday lives, that which we are.

Well, that's the planets, so let's get back to the moon. We know that it affects the tide of the sea and we also know there are a lot of fluids that make up part of our bodies. So it's no surprise to find out that it affects us too. If we were able to flow with life again, things wouldn't be so bad. But not only society puts us out of rhythm with the moon. We also take hormonal birth control and use artificial light when in darkness. All these things put us out of sync with what should be our natural flow. You see the moon like us women, has a 28 day cycle, as it takes 28 days to circle the earth. Every two weeks during these 28 days when it is in line with the sun and the earth, gravities pull on the earth is at its strongest.

The new moon is the first phase when the moon is nearest to the sun. (Strongest gravity pull)

The first quarter moon is the first quarter that the moon travels round the earth.

(Weakest gravity pull)

Full moon is when the moon is furthest away from the sun. (Strongest gravity pull)

Last quarter moon is when the moon and sun form a 90 degree axis. (Weakest gravity pull).

To simplify, picture the earth as the center of a clock face and the moon travelling around the outside anti clockwise. The new moon is at 12, the first quarter is at 9 or quarter to the full moon at 6 or half past, and the last quarter is at 3 or a quarter past.

So if the tide has its ebb and flow and were resisting ours, no wonder were all over the show.

So how much more out there in the universe, actually affects our being?

Nature is so important to our being and yet were becoming more and more disconnected from it, hiding away in buildings watching TV and playing video games. Jumping in cars to get from A to B. We exercise more and more in gyms instead of in natural surroundings. We do all this then wonder why we're in desperate need for a holiday. We get over tired, we sleep through the day and before we know it our body clock is upside down. The sun is our energy, the air is our breath, the water our fluid and the earth our body. So it stands to reason that we need them to survive. Without it we lose the ability to flow in its rhythm. When we stop flowing in life's rhythm we either go to slow or too fast. When we go to slow we become stagnant and miss out on the true abundance of life and all it has to offer. We come to a standstill in our lives which isn't fulfilling our need to growing and evolve. This can lead to bitterness as we watch others pass us by. We can get jealous of others achievements instead of feeling pleased that they are doing well. It can lead to bitterness towards ourselves and feelings of insecurity and a whole load of other emotions. We can become depressed because everything is being held down and not being dealt with, or we can go to fast and just like when we're driving on roads. We can cause mishaps and accidents to slow us down, or we get so far so quick then something stops us until the universal flow has a chance to catch up. We can take on stress after stress until we become ill and have to stop while we get better. A big thing that has held us back in life, is fear. When we are not in the flow of life, we cause things to go wrong. When this happens we start to become afraid of things happening again, which they inevitably do due to the fact that we are not flowing in life's synchronicity. If we do not deal with these situations or release the stress and anxiety of them. These fears can build up to the point of in-trepidation where we become stuck and too afraid to move forward in life, which can then develop into phobias.

I started out as a very quiet child and spoke very little, if at all. Living in my own little imaginative safe world. As I got older and started to communicate with people I became easily embarrassed, as I wasn't used to the attention that received when speaking to people. As a teenager my hormones were all over the place, because I had kept everything quiet and inside of me. So all my emotions that had been held down, needed a release. I found that I was very imbalanced and was either too quiet or too loud. When I found myself center of attention, it wasn't enough and I needed more. So I would carry things on too far, causing me embarrassment from another perspective.

Fear is more complex than we realise and if not dealt with early on can become a difficult barrier to break down. It can start so small and yet build so big. This is because we have wonderful vivid imaginations that create our world around us. Fear is a negative energy and needs a positive to balance it out. If you love something it is hard to be afraid of it. Therefore where love is, fear cannot exist. This is because love balances fear out back to being a warning signal in order to keep us safe. We ourselves create fear, which means we ourselves are actually in control of it. Now we never said it would be easy and it won't happen overnight, but if your body can be tipped out of balance. Then it sure can be put back in balance. Scientists prove this more and more by finding cures for things we never thought possible. The only discrepancy with medicine is that it only cures the immediate problem and so far does not seem to treat the cause. For example, with tonsillitis the cause affects the tonsils. Medicine can be used to treat the tonsils, however because the cause hasn't been cured or treated. The effects can be sore, inflamed, swollen tonsils which can reoccur. Sometimes to the point of the tonsils being removed. So far the cause can only be removed from ourselves by ourselves, but it can be helped by such things as massage and other holistic therapies. These assist the lymphatic system in detoxing the body and therefore cleansing it and releasing negative energy.

If we don't deal with these causes they will build up on top of each other and the emotions that are caused get pushed down further and further, layer upon layer until they become depressed emotions.

Here is where depression comes in. Even depressed feelings need a release, which is why people end up with depression. Depression is happening more and more and in younger people. A main cause of this is the virtual reality word that we live in, we constantly watch films and horror movies that cause us fear. Yet we sit there and suppress the feelings with no actual physical outlet, other than the overspill of emotions in the form of tears. We don't physically fight back and we do not run away, so the emotions we have just taken on are suppressed in the body.

More and more children are playing virtual reality games which involve fighting and wars, not only just on TVs but on hand held games and phones as it becomes a constant way of life. The adrenaline rush that these cause become addictive. However because it is only virtual reality, we are not releasing the adrenaline in a physical way. Advancing technology itself, is a wonderful and amazing accomplishment. If used in a positive manner it can be extremely helpful and beneficial. When used wrongly in the manner that we have mentioned, it affects us greatly as our body accepts all the emotions as reality and does not know the difference between realities and make believe. The brain is clever enough to create this technology and it also has the power to create our lives around us. Our brains are so advanced, that when we constantly feed ourselves with a certain vibration. We then send out that thought wave that we are focused on, out into the world to attract more of the same. So we can now see by simply watching the wrong programs and playing the wrong games, we are doing ourselves more harm than good. The negative frequency will come back to us in 'reality' causing us to crave that same adrenaline rush we have received from the technology we have been used to. The depressed feelings need to find a release. Many people may turn to drugs, alcohol, cigarettes or other because it gives a similar adrenaline rush, or fills in the void when not receiving the same adrenaline rush. Doing this takes us out of the real world as we know it and suppresses our real feelings further. What we don't realise is we are sending ourselves further into depression and getting addicted to poisonous toxins, harming our bodies. We get into such an imbalanced state, that it is hard to see where the actual cause is coming from.

Supposing we have parents or people around us who are constantly negative. Who have their own challenges in showing their love and affection? As a youngster we have enough problems understanding our own behaviour, let alone our parents. So rather than deal with it, we may find an escape by playing game stations. Burying ourselves in a completely different world, or are we? You see we start fighting virtual battles instead of the real thing. So here's the thing... We just focused on all the negative of the situation around us, which as we know from the law of attraction is a vibrational thought that brings back more of the same. So not only are we getting more of the same in reality, but we are now focusing on stressful situations in games. Except with this, there is no real physical outlet for the emotions we feel whist playing. The aggression builds within whilst the focus of attention, creates even more of the same in our real world. When we come back into the real world and confront that which we have hidden from (as the situations don't go away until we deal with them). We are not ready to deal with them, so the pent up aggression comes out in uncontrollable outbursts and much frustration.

If we have a problem, we have to deal with it. We must confront it and find out why we feel the way we do deep down. Only when we can understand it and stop any habits formed as a way of protecting ourselves, can we let it go. If we choose to ignore it, the problem will just get bigger and bigger until we can take no more, we are then either forced to deal with it or become ill or at dis-ease in one way or another.

As we have already said, the whole point of our being is to evolve. One of our main challenges when evolving is to be able to balance our ego. To do this we have to balance the mind, body and soul as we do with our whole being. The ego is such a difficult aspect of ourselves to control, as it needs to be strong enough to drive us forward but too much can cause problems. We now know that fear protects us, but too much fear can hold us back. At the opposite end of the scale the ego drives us forward, but too much ego can cause an addiction with a need for power, greed, control and a feeling of greatness. There is nothing wrong in wanting for things or wanting to better ourselves and our lives, as the kingdom of god knows only of pure abundance. It is we ourselves who limit ourselves and hold ourselves back feeling that we do not deserve the riches of life, due to the habits we have formed in order to protect ourselves as we have gone through life. To know yourself completely is to understand yourself and accept yourself, warts and all without judgement. This is to see yourself how God sees you. When you can do this completely you can then see the true being of everyone else. To see people in this way diminishes fear, as enemy's can only be seen with love and understanding. When the ego is out of balance we do not see ourselves clearly. Therefore we cannot understand others. We get hooked on the need to feel in control. In a pure state of being we do not need to control ourselves, we just are. Therefore we do not need to control others. When we get hooked, we need to constantly fight for our position and always need to be on top or above everyone else. When we fall, the old emotions such as jealousy arise. As we don't like this feeling we fight with our ego to get back on top again. This will never give us satisfaction because we are not using our own energy to be on top, we are using other peoples. Wanting to be the best that we can be for ourselves uses our own energy and means we can happily accept those doing better. Needing to be better than others, is not wanting the best for everyone and therefore is negative behavior.

Because the ego is such a strong part of our being, it is very easy to get hooked on its negative characteristics such as a need to control. This can be controlling ourselves or others, or even things around us. This is why we have so much bullying going on in the world. It can be something as simple as wanting to have better clothes as your friends, or better technology than your neighbour. It can go as far as wanting to beat a competitor rather than just wanting to win for yourself and in its extremes people who want to control their community, rather than do their best for the people in it. You can see and feel when someone's ego is not balanced by the way they treat others. They give off a feeling of importance and may make you feel beneath them. Another extremity is where people following their beliefs and religions, use control to try and force others to believe that their teachings are the right way and the only way. Therefore condemning everyone else's beliefs that differ from their own. A religion is in place to give us understanding of life and its universal flow i.e. the law of attraction, teaching us how to strive to be good and also the consequences of being bad. Religions themselves do not condemn us for getting things wrong, as we have to learn the bad alongside the good. To know the bad in life helps us to know what we don't want in order to know what we do want, allowing us free will to make our own choices. It is the people who teach, who sometimes get it wrong by letting their ego take over and try to use control. We are all guilty of this from time to time, as we are all learning to balance ourselves. None of us are perfect here on earth due to the forces of nature and gravity that pull on our male and female energies. Nobody should feel fear from a religion that they are part of. If what is around you is of pure love, light and goodness, then the feelings you have within yourself should feel wonderful and uplifting.

The more we get hooked on the feelings of control within the ego, the more diverse the feelings can become. Being in control gives us a feeling of power. The more power we have, the more we want. Money contributes to this a great deal, we lose sight of the reality of money being a way of means to exchange goods. When we start to see money as the richness of life itself instead of the bargaining tool that it is, we get hooked on the feelings of greed. This is because the more we feel we have, the more in control we feel giving us a greater feeling of power. We forget that the true abundance in life, is that which we have and enjoy in our lives. It is not what we own. The reason we feel we need to own is to gain control, which comes from our own fears and insecurities. When we stop sharing what we have and we stop giving out, we stop the flow of abundance that comes back to us. So look around you. At the nice things you own, your beautiful home, your nice car parked out front or anything else you happen to have. Do you own them, need to have them and want for more. Or do you have them, truly appreciate and enjoy them? There is a big difference between being rich in goods and being rich in life. Which is why some people with very little are richer than some of those who have a lot of material items. Do you actually realise how much you have, enough to enjoy it? If you don't see and feel the abundance of what you have now, when you get what you want it will still feel the same. A poor person who on receiving a coin who feels excited and grateful is richer than a rich person, who is given a note or a cheque which means nothing or very little to him/her. The saying that money is the route of all evil is not exactly true. It is our attitudes toward money that can become the route for evil, not the money itself. We can also give so much to others but still block the flow of abundance. This can happen if we have grown up with a mindset of feeling unworthy and undeservedly of the gifts that are bestowed upon us. So when people offer to pay for us and others try to give to us, we politely refuse as we feel guilty taking from them and therefore push away the flow of abundance or the gifts that life has to offer. Many of us don't truly see what's in front of us. When we go to work we focus on the money that we will receive in the pay packets, instead of focusing on the love of service that we are able to do for others.

Specific fields of work attract more people with bigger egos than people with a more balanced ego, due to the nature of the job. Specifically managerial jobs and jobs with authority. When we go to work we should be going into a job that we truly love and enjoy, everything else will come to us. What we need is not necessarily in the form of money. Business in life has become a viscous circle, people are working at Jobs that aren't satisfying because they are focusing on the need for money. Sometimes our fears often concerning money, hold us back from moving forward in life. We feel trapped in the job we are in when it does not fulfil us, yet we are afraid to leave for fear of failure. Afraid that what we truly want, won't appear or provide enough for our needs. This is down to our own fears that we create. This is why the law of attraction works positively abundant for some of us and not for others. Others have stopped working altogether rather than doing jobs that aren't fulfilling them and their lives, accepting a smaller payment to live basic and possibly what they think is some freedom. In time these people do not feel free, but instead feel trapped. They are unable to work at anything they love for fear of losing the dependency that they have left. To do what we love doesn't always provide enough money to actually work, as more costs are involved to go to work than to stay at home. It takes recessions and such like to pull things slightly back into line. The whole situation has been started with good intention, by providing a life line for those in need who are unable or find difficulty in supporting themselves. It went wrong when the balance was tipped too far, people in work found themselves paying more and more to support those in need. The problem is not the giving and receiving, it is the fact that people do not have a choice. Because they do not have free will they start to try and gain back control by holding back what they have and becoming reluctant to give and share. Because people are holding back and trying to take back what belongs to them, the ego causes us to lose sight of the need to just balance ourselves. We then tip the balance the opposite way, by starting to take from others that which is not rightfully ours. This causes a knock on effect of mistrust and sets the same pattern off in someone else. This is why too many people in business feel they have to be ruthless and in control, rather than relaxing into kindness and generosity.

If money was not an issue, what would you do right now?

When it comes down to it we are all the same and all doing our best some are more advanced in some ways and others have learnt more in other ways. Which is why we have no right to judge each other, as none of us perfect in every aspect of our lives. In other words we are all the same and all equal.

HEALING THE MIND AND BODY

Well we now have some kind of understanding as to what we put our minds through on a daily basis. We can see how easily our mind and bodies have been tipped out of balance. Bringing ourselves back into balance is rather like a set of scales. We can tip back and forth until we get it right.

So where do we start

The beginning starts the same way for everyone which is good intention to get well to be balanced, or to be a better person. It doesn't matter as long as it is for your highest good. The journey will be different for each individual, as every symptom has been created by different causes and had different effects. There are many methods of healing, all those mentioned can be used and can work alongside each other. We should all use the methods that are right for us at the time. A good starting point is to focus on the one thing that is biggest to you at this point in time. Whether it be your weight, your diet, your health. It could even be your sleep patterns or migraines. (For me it was a case of I just wanted to be a better person). You may be taken in a different direction and may have to heal other things first, before the main thing you wish to heal. This happens because the smaller things, may be part of the cause of the bigger concern. We often try to change our diet in order to change our weight, however there may be something deeper that is causing us to eat wrongly in the first place. This is why many people after losing weight regain what they lost, other things need to be released to get to the main cause. When we know what we want and make a conscious decision, the universe responds. It is when we cannot decide and are in two minds as to which way to go or what to do, that nothing happens. When making a conscious decision to heal a part of the self and perhaps thinking of trying a massage. Do not refuse without good reason, when someone appears offering something different like a self help book for instance or an opportunity to go to a yoga class. The universe knows exactly what we need, better than we do. Just go with the flow through the doors that open. Learn to listen to your instinct and you will know if you're in sync with life. Therefore you will know if things feel right or not. If we slow down, we really don't need to fight everything in our path. Don't panic if you're in a habit of thinking negatively. Just relax and replace it with positive thoughts. The more you think positive the more the negative thoughts will fall away. The more positive you put out, the more it comes back to you.

The most important and effective way to heal the body, is the simplest. It is the very first thing we do when we are born. Breathe. Who'd of thought it! Breathing is the most essential part of life. It not only keeps us functioning, it releases stress and yet many of us don't breathe correctly. When we have a fright we often hold our breath or when we get hay fever some of us start to breathe through our mouths instead of our noses.

Breathing is the one thing I stopped doing correctly from a young age. As a child I developed allergic rhinitis. For those of you who haven't yet come across this, 1 sneezed a lot. I'm not sure which caused me to sneeze first, dust, cats, dogs, perfume. The more my nose reacted ready to sneeze, the more I breathed through my mouth instead of my nose. The less I used my nose, the worse it got. Over time the tablets I took stopped working and I would have to find something else. Eventually I developed hay fever as well and started to have injections as well as tablets. It was only when I discovered reiki that I was able to start getting better. As time went on I used many other methods alongside the reiki and I'm now happy to say I don't take tablets or injections, I now breathe through my nose. Although allergies and hay fever affected my breathing, they weren't the only things. As a teenager I was taught to stand up straight with shoulders back, stomache in and all that. What I didn't realise was that holding my stomache in constantly, wasn't allowing me to breathe properly. Instead I was taking short shallow breaths, preventing the necessary amount of oxygen needed for me to function properly. I would often have dizzy spells. Whichever method I have used, I have always found breathing to be an important part of releasing the stress. I have since learnt that if I deep breathe 12 times at night to release the 12 hours of stress taken on during the day. Then 12 times in the morning to release the 12 hours of stress taken on during the night. I actually don't pick up viruses like I used to. I only seem to become ill when I get really stressed for some reason. More often than not, if I feel that I am coming down with something. I can usually fight it off with deep breathing and rest.

As over 50% of our bodies are made up of water, it stands to reason that drinking water is the best way to cleanse the body. This is why many practitioners offer a glass of water straight after a treatment. We are like walking batteries that constantly drain and need topping up. We need recharging with food and water, which brings us on to the most problematic... Food. What do we eat? What don't we eat?

I've watched friends who have been on one diet after another, never sticking to them longer than a few months and always putting the weight back on. Personally I think fresh food that has just been picked is the best, I believe a little of everything does you good and too much of anything is not good. Everything in moderation. It all comes down to balance again. I haven't quite mastered this one yet, but my eating habits are changing for the better slowly but surely. The one thing I have learnt is to stop beating myself up when I slip into old eating habits. Instead I enjoy it, slowly bringing myself back to better eating habits little and often.

I have found that cutting something out altogether, just makes me crave for it after a week or two. It is always better to change things slowly where possible, giving the mind and body chance to adapt to the changes.

Being set by constant time limits hasn't helped our eating habits. The fact is we should eat when we are hungry. Eat slowly and stop when we feel satisfied. We all too often go past feeling hungry and either don't want to eat, or eat too fast missing the satisfied signal by over eating. The more we do this, failing to listen to our bodies. The more we eat, resulting in being overweight. Or we don't eat enough, skip to many meals resulting in being under weight. We seem to have got so used to rushing around, that we find it hard to slow down to sit and enjoy what we eat.

Exercise is a great way to tone up the body, burn off excess fat and build up an adrenaline rush that can help release toxins from the body. However many of us start to exercise and before we know it slide back into old habits, this is because exercise is a mind set and not just a bodily function. Whatever causes of stress built up over time to slow us down, need to be released for us to become more active again.

When we have massage we go to relieve aches and pains, wanting to release knots and tension from our bodies. This works well when our bodies are ready to release and let go of the stress but when we haven't yet found the root cause, the same tension builds and two weeks or so later we are back again wanting to relieve the same tense muscles. This is because these pains in our body have taken years to develop and cannot be released over night. Each time we receive a massage it loosens blockages, enough for a small amount to be released before clogging back up again. Using other methods of therapy alongside, can help the release to be slightly bigger and quicker. A great example of this is my youngest daughter Fern. At a very young age Fern was taught to massage by her aunty. She was so tiny she hadn't got the strength to give a proper massage, but the healing that flowed through her hands because of her loving intent was amazing. Had she carried on to become a masseur, her kind loving nature would have excelled her just as it does with everything else that she does? Over time the more that is released the more enlightened we become and therefore release more, faster. This can be said for all ways of healing as the more we remove the clearer we can see. Also the more enlightened we become, the more we've actually learnt. This then speeds the process further as the more we know, the more we can learn and faster. Allowing the release of old unlearned patterns that clogged our bodies up in the first place.

Acupuncture focuses on the pressure points in the body, which release the flow of energy. Rather like an egg when we put a hole at either end, so that one releases the pressure for the contents to flow through. As the energy flows around the whole body. Certain points are connected to certain parts of the body. This again takes time as with massage, as the body will only let go of that which it is ready to release.

Yoga is a technique working in a similar way by using positions and breathing to release the flow of energy. Once learnt, we can do this for ourselves. The more the body learns to relax with breath, the further we can stretch our bodies to release the blockages. You may hear the odd clicking sound as parts of the body relax back into their natural state. This is because we have to use force to hold tension in our bodies, so to release it we have to learn to relax and let go.

Tai chi is an art of learning to feel the flow of energy around us, by using mind and body to feel and move the energy surrounding the outer perimeter of our being. It teaches us the ability to flow the energy through our bodies. We can also build up positive energy around us as a protective shield against negativity. It also helps us to relax the mind, flowing in line with life's universal flow and synchronicity. The one thing we all should be doing and yet seem to have lost the ability to do.

Reiki is a form of hands on healing and is a way of speeding up the bodies own natural ability to heal. We liken this to prayer as both ask for the highest good from a loving state of mind. Reiki and healing focus on the inner body, helping the body to release stress. While prayer is more openly used for people and circumstances surrounding them. The stigma comes when people think that reiki practitioners and healers are playing God.

As a reiki practitioner myself, we are taught to be humble and are in service of others out of loving kindness. From experience the more love I can feel for a client the stronger the healing seems to be.

It works on positive vibration which will stop flowing if used with ill intent as with tai chi, the mind is the main force behind the healing. The use of symbols help to strengthen the healing. When drawn and spoken they become even stronger. This is because they all have a vibration. This can work well alongside all other therapies. The clients own higher mind is always in control of how much or how little, if any at all healing is received.

Meditation is a relaxed state of mind. Using a deep breathing technique to relax the body and mind, allowing the higher mind to take over. A guided meditation can be used to guide the mind to release things, or to reprogram the mind to a healthier state. Hypnosis works in a very similar way. The person being hypnotized is always in control as to how far they relax into a trance like condition.

Mediumship works in a similar way by relaxing into an altered state, allowing the self to connect with the universal flow via the higher mind (gut instinct and knowing). The universal energy is where all the information comes from, due to the fact that we are all connected and universal energy flows through all. Past, present and future. This is hard to accept unless experienced, or understood from a scientist's perspective.

Tarot cards, angel cards, runes, pendulums, psychometric, tea leaves, and crystal balls are all aids to help mediumship. They can act as a starting block to get energy flowing and ease the communication process. As with phone calls we can sometimes get an unclear line. The more we connect the clearer the line becomes. It is simply a case of developing our gut or basic instincts by using them. The more we use our instincts, the more they work. The key is to learn to relax and allow the information to flow. To force or to try and control what you hear will not work.

Many of us often use telepathy without realising it. One of my best friend abroad. We can go for months without speaking and yet when one decides to contact the other, you can almost guarantee that the other person was already thinking of them. I've lost count of numbers of times I've guessed who is texting me before picking up my phone.

Colour is a big part of our lives and just as the sunlight holds within it a rainbow of colours. So does the pure white light (i.e. Energy) that runs through our bodies. This is why we have an aura of colour surrounding our bodies. If practiced, some people are able to relax their vision enough to see some of the colours. This is easiest done if there is a plain white background behind the person you are looking at, each colour just like everything else has its own vibration. This is why a rainbow always appears with the colours in the same order. When focusing on a colour for long enough, it can affect our mood. Yellow is very uplifting and can make us feel happy. While red which is great for energy if we absorb too much, it can make us feel angry. This is why we all prefer different colours for different things. We may be drawn to that which we lack in our bodies. A great way to use colour in healing is with meditation, visualizing each colour in turn filling your energy centers. There are many guided meditations in stores and online which can help you do this.

Essential oils, are oils taken from plants and things on the earth. To see the beautiful colours that some of these can form, take a look at aura soma. This is a colour therapy which uses its colour to treat the body and also to give readings similar to tarot cards. The oils can be used at certain parts of the body according to their qualities. The aromas can be breathed in and work on different aspects of our being. With normal essential oils they must be used carefully as per instructions due to their concentration. Some can be used in the bath, others in massage and some can also be used with the breath.

Crystals are a special kind of rock or solid material where the molecules come together in a repeating formation. The pattern causes them to form in unique shapes. Crystals form from the earth when liquid rock cools. Certain crystals such as quartz are used for their vibration, as when an electrical current is sent through. It has a very precise vibration and is great for keeping time in watches. Diamonds are the hardest substance on earth and are used in tools. Crystals are used in jewellery not only because of their beauty, but due to their healing properties when next to the skin. Using their colours to match with our energy centers in the body, they can have strong healing abilities and also help with enlightenment. Helping us to access the information concerning ourselves from our higher mind

Of course we cannot do a better job than the earth itself.

I was once given a piece of aloe vera straight from the plant, to rub on my sunburn once the acid had been rinsed away in water. I've never felt relief so good. Since then I have tried almost every aloe vera treatment on the market and nothing comes close.

We are made from the dust of the earth, so what better healer than the earth itself and what better medicine than all the gifts it provides in their natural state.

However this does not dismiss the amazing works of doctors, nurses, chemists etc.

I myself only recently turned to the doctor for help and medication to use for a more immediate effect for my symptoms of depression. I understood my condition and on feeling the effects could possibly heal myself from its cause a lot quicker without the medication. The problem was that I had to live alongside others who didn't understand my condition. So to be fair to myself and others, 1 asked for help. I know that using drugs long term is not a cure and can have knock on effects causing other problems, but as we progress. More and more doctors are opening up to the ideas of alternative medicine. These people with all their knowledge and training are very valuable to the healing profession. I have had the experience of a professor in medicine diverting into holistic therapies and healing. The work he does is amazing and I learnt a lot from him. Using other peoples healing abilities alongside my own, has proven to be very powerful indeed. The operations that are performed these days, are amazing considering the complexity of the human body. They have given people a starting process, for their own healing abilities to take over from. The results of which are astounding. People who were thought never to recover have literally walked out of hospitals. Abilities proven with science help strengthen our own belief system, giving us the strength and power to go on to heal ourselves.

When we know that we will recover, no one can tell us different. My brother in law at a younger age had a horrific car accident, he was taken to hospital and had to be resuscitated three times. He broke every bone in his legs and was told he would never walk again. At the time he was making his way to be a professional boxer. We can only imagine the hurt he would have felt. Thinking that he had not only lost his profession, but his hobby and passion all at once. He is the kind of man that knows what he knows and knows what he wants. He's strong willed and nobody can tell him any different. So when the surgeon told him he would never walk again, he refused to believe it. He said he would walk out of the hospital and that's exactly what he did. You see we have our own knowing and if we listen to it we can make anything possible. Who's to say, where would he be now had he listened to the negative news. He might be in a wheel chair right now, but instead. He not only walked again, he ran, drove, cycled and made his way back into the boxing ring.

My Healing Journey So Far:

I think my first method of healing was possibly the bible. I had a pocket book which showed me where to look for comfort and guidance for different things that were going on in my life. I know some schools use this method for children in schools who are perhaps being bullied or struggling for some reason. This led me to asking God for help in certain areas of my life through prayer. What came next, was the help I had asked for in totally unexpected ways. I started to come across self-help books, each one giving just the right information that I needed at the time. Then in January 2006 my nan who was my last living grandparent, passed away. I woke having had a crazy dream leaving a knot in my stomach and I guess I just knew she was saying goodbye. Not long after, I received the disheartening phone call. After the funeral I started to visit her grave, just to sit and chat. Each time I felt as though someone was walking up behind me. I'd turn around constantly looking for someone. Feeling uneasy each time, I would leave without having spoken a word. It was then my ex-husband decided I should go and see his aunty, who was a medium. I'd never experienced a clairvoyant before, but as I knew his aunt well I thought why not. I remember to this day, the first thing she said to me. She told me everything that she already knew and explained that as it was still so soon after her passing that she may not come through as she may be going through some healing on the other side. We went to a small sunny room where she liked to work from. She made the connection, sure enough Nan and a few others came through. One I knew and one I didn't know, who was confirmed to me later by my mum. She must have spent about 3 hours telling me all sorts of things, including things that only I knew. She even told me things I didn't know, so that I could go and check it out for myself. I suddenly felt a disconnection just as aunty Josie said, "There leaving us with that". Well we carried on chatting and saying our thank you's but the whole time it was just niggling at me to ask her to teach me. I suddenly blurted it out. "Teach you what?" She asked. "Everything you know I said. "I'm not sure I can, it's taken me 30 years. Let me think about it and get back to you." Well the next evening, she phoned me all excited saying "I have your first lesson ready," We never looked back. One day each week we would spend a day together, while she taught me everything she knew. This is where my healing really swung into action. We went on to do courses together, sharing information and books. We even held a class ourselves at one stage. She went on to teach me healing and became my much loved reiki master. She had taught me everything she knew. Then one day in 2009 It was her time to return home (as she'd always put it). It was a tough time for many as she was much loved and greatly missed. Josie had taught me that life goes on and we set to work together Josie on one dimension and me on the other, doing our best to help those left behind suffering her loss.

Well as I uncover the depths of my being, I realise I'm not such a bad person after all. In fact I'm actually starting to quite like myself. As this is happening I'm starting to notice that I don't push people away so much anymore. As I change in my personality so do the pains and ailments of my body. As some pains disappear for good, it allows others to surface ready for me to deal with. The one thing I notice is that as I remove the thick stubborn walls that I built up over the years, the more sensitive 1 become. I am more easily upset by smaller things. This is ok as the bigger things either don't upset me or just don't happen anymore. With all this comes a knowing and understanding, so there really is no need for fear. Talking of fear, it is one of the things I'm dealing with right now. On the left side of my back I have dull pain which I know to be my fears, caused by things going wrong as I have pushed out of the flow of life. On the right side of my back I have a dull pain caused from fighting to protect myself from my fears. I know this as the more I listen to my body, the more I hear. Sometimes we all just seem to know things and trust me, we're not wrong. Ever said to yourself, I just knew that was going to happen. I know plenty who have, and if you have well that's what they call claircognizance. (Knowing without knowing how you know). It's basically using your instincts or being aware of that gut feeling we all have from time to time. The more we use it, the more it develops. Clairsentience is sensing things by touch which most of us healers develop. Clairaudience is an ability to hear voices, by developing the inner ear. Clairvoyance is a development of the third eye in order to see images in a dream like state. We are all capable of developing these senses. Getting back to my fears. I'm now at a stage of once again reprogramming my brain. I constantly tell myself that I do not need to fight any more to protect my fears. I tell my fear that I do not need to be afraid any more, as I am now moving forward in the flow of life's synchronicity. Eventually on realising that I am more in flow than out, my body will respond to my brain and release the pain. With perhaps a little help along the way. You see on trying out all the healing methods we have spoken about. I have come to realise that they all work in a very similar way, but each have their own qualities and can assist each other greatly.

Well I still have a long way to go, but I have to say that I have gone from being a very unhappy person on the inside and an overly happy person on the outside to being very happy, calm, content on both the inside and outside. The more balanced I become the more genuinely happy and content I feel. The more things just fall into place in my life in everyday things. When you hear your friends moaning because no matter how late you arrive to pick your kids up from school, you always get a good parking space. You know the law of attraction is working for you. I see things from a different perspective now, yet I still believe and understand that which I learnt along the way. You see it's all the same, just from a different angle. God and the angels helped me to understand the scientific view. The scientists view on things helps me understand the bigger picture. All points of view are necessary.

<u>HEAVEN ON EARTH</u>

What's the point to all this... If we were able to heal ourselves totally, removing all the stress taken on during this life time back to a balanced state. We should also have the knowledge to stay pretty balanced. Not only from that which we have learned here on earth. We should also then be able to relax our minds, in order to access our higher mind which has access to Infinite knowledge. The more we find out about how everything works and how everything was created. The more we can accept that all these crazy ideas that we have really do work. So healing with a force that we cannot actually see and accessing information that others fall to hear see or sense, becomes much more acceptable. This is all due to the fact that we can actually start to understand how it can be possible. We are a very complicated existence and even now, we still have many unanswered questions. The reason we need to get back to a balanced state, is so we can experience true abundance.

Picture this. You're born into a loving family with more love than you know what to do with. You feel as special as every other person on the planet. Everything you see around you is shared equally, so you never experience jealousy. Everyone around you is loving, giving and caring, as is everyone you meet through life. Because of this there is no lack of necessities, because everyone shares. Therefore everyone has the same and there is no need to be better than anyone in any way. Everyone goes with the flow and arrives to work or wherever they are going just at the perfect time. Breaks are taken as and when needed whether it be to eat play, exercise or rest. Accidents don't happen because you're in touch with your gut instinct and so have the knowledge to avoid them. You enjoy everything that life has to offer. It's almost like you're a child experiencing everything for the first time. The wind against your face, the sun glistening through the trees. The beautiful aromas from flowers and plants and the list goes on. Is this heaven on earth?

What is it that we are all looking for? Isn't it heaven on earth without arguments and bad feelings? Without hurt, pain and suffering. Is it possible for us to even get to such a balanced state that heaven on earth could even exist? We probably won't really know until we get there. Possibly we will heal ourselves and gravity will not have the same pull on us, but hopefully we will be able to balance ourselves with its forces. Allowing ourselves to have compassionate feelings whilst keeping ourselves detached from the situations. Keeping control of all negative emotions, anger and jealousy becoming things of the past.

To help us understand all this, let's start at the very beginning. The Big Bang. As far as we know everything that exists today was so compressed to such a density that what exists now hadn't actually formed. Just like us, it grew (expanded) and as it did it created. Just as we are still expanding and creating so is the Big Bang, (the beginning of time, Gods creation. It's still expanding and accelerating. On our comfy little planet earth we've learnt to understand the concept of time and space that we need to help us in our daily existence or so we think. We may follow the time on a clock, but that doesn't stop time going faster for some and slower for others. Even that which we know about time has developed along with our knowledge as we realised the earth was round and others were experiencing night time as we were experiencing daylight but outside of this it seems that absolutely anything is possible. Time bending time going back on itself, time going faster in one place yet slower in another. We don't know the half of it which is why when people tell me that such things as teleporting, invisibility and other crazy ideas on TV aren't possible. Although they may be right at this moment in time, I tend to disagree. From my perspective I believe absolutely that if we can come up with the idea, then we can come up with the reality if we so choose. What amuses me is that we watch things on TV in our homes, yet they are actually happening on the other side of the world at the same time. So how on earth can that be possible? By someone's crazy miraculous idea brought into reality? Just because we can't prove our theory today, doesn't mean we can't create it tomorrow, next week, next year and so on.

The universe was so hot and dense that as it expanded, it cooled and as it cooled it went on to create. We know that if we heat food it changes such as a soup that thickens and as it cools it changes again. It can separate leaving a thick soup with a watery residue. If everything is in place therefore the right temperatures and humidity etc. it goes on to breed bacteria. Chemicals can change from gases to liquids and then to solids. So in actual fact everything can change, evolve, adapt, grow, create, there are no limits. So I guess we are similar to a bacteria that has grown, developed and is still doing so. It doesn't matter if we came about here on earth, or our building blocks of life started earlier before the planet was formed. The fact is we came from that hot dense soup we call the Big Bang. So if everything and all of us started from the same point growing from each other, then we are in fact one as a whole. It stands to reason that we need to live on, survive from and heal with all of that which created us in the first place.

We look pretty solid right, we even feel solid. Yet break us down under a microscope and were made up of so many particles. Scientists are now finding that those particles are made up of even smaller particles and so on. Yes you've all heard the names before (protons, neutrons and quarks etc.)

I won't pretend, I have a real job trying to get my head around all this scientific stuff. Even though I don't fully understand it, I find it fascinating. However I find it much easier to experience it from within than to learn all the facts and figures. Having all this information to hand, helps me understand how my experiences can be possible from my experience, when we can manage to relax every muscle in our bodies. We can feel all those particles that we are made up of vibrate when we are in this state, we actually let go of pain. I used to have treatment for my jaw which used to lock constantly when I relaxed to the point of letting go completely, my jaw fell back into its natural alignment and the pain disappeared. The problem is learning to stay that way. The moment I stopped what I was doing everything tightened up again. I know, that as a child I felt nearer to that feeling than I do now. So all I have to do now, is release the stress that I've taken on and held in my body since birth. This is where all the healing methods that we've mentioned come in. There may be more, but I can only tell you about the ones I know about and have experienced in life.

To help us understand a little more. Everything we see has a vibrational frequency which is very similar. Because we are all similar, we appear solid. Vibrate at a totally different frequency and we become invisible. A great example is a propeller on an aeroplane. It looks solid as it slowly starts to spin, but as it speeds up it appears to go backwards. As it speeds up even more it then starts to become transparent. We not only have a vibrational frequency, we also contain colour. Not just the colour of our hair and skin, but a rainbow of colour. This is the same rainbow prism of colour produced by the sun. Each colour at a slightly different frequency causing it to appear in the same sequence of colour each time we see it. So if the sun contains these colours within its pure white light then so must we, as we have the same pure white light (energy) running through us. This is why we need the sun as part of our energy source. We absorb it's nutrients through the skin, which is why we feel brighter, happier and more energetic in summer. If colour makes up a part of our very existence, then it should be able to repair any damage done to that part of us during our lifetime. We all use colour, but do we really pay attention to the reasons why we do. Do we notice the affects colour has on the way we feel? Most of us go for a nice cool calming blue or green in the kitchen, as it can become a hot stressful environment Walk into a bright yellow room and it gives us a happy lift. Whereas a splash of red or orange in a bedroom can make us feel sexy. However too much of this colour for too long can draw out more anger than passion for some of us, or boost our energy for others. Of course how much each colour affects us is different for each of us, depending on those colours which our body needs.

If we think about our bodies and those parts of us that can be seen by the naked eye. We realise just how complicated we are. How the heart pumps to flow blood through our veins, how our digestive system breaks down and uses that which it needs to function. Our eyes adjust to light and dark, whilst our nose breathes in oxygen from the air to fill our lungs. Thus acting like pumps taking oxygen to where it's needed and releasing gasses that are not. If we cut ourselves or damage ourselves in any way, our bodies naturally repair themselves where possible. We do all this without so much as a thought. Amazing isn't it we are made up of so many parts that we can see. Put all that under a microscope and we can see that those parts are made up of even smaller parts which doesn't stop there. When we get to the tiniest things that we can't even see. Some of these things aren't just contained in our body, but also are outside of our body and not only that but they interconnect with everything else that we connect with this is how we absorb what we need from the sun's rays and the atmosphere through the skin. It is also how mediums and others pick up information.

It is how healers can heal someone close to them and also someone on the other side of the world, having never even met. All that is needed is some kind of connection, as simple as a tiny thought wave. As we are still evolving and the Big Bang hasn't actually stopped, we can connect to information that is still in the past and also that which is in the future. Mind blowing isn't it. So if everything is interconnected as one, we are all like little cogs in a well-oiled machine. Working away at something much bigger and we all have an effect. Look again and we are like machines working bigger machines with even smaller machines inside us, working us. Wow where does it end. We are the universe and the universe is in us. The building blocks that created the universe are the same building blocks that created us, which are the same building blocks that we use to create more things and so on. Our mind moulds all that is and if you think you have your own mind, think again because every mind affects every other mind. So is it one big mind with lots of different cogs? How often do we find ourselves thinking along the lines of someone else's thoughts? Did their mind influence mine, or did my mind influence theirs. Are things like this just coincidence? We don't believe so. If matter exists only with mind to control it, then everything is planned from the very beginning of time. Things can alter as time goes on, but it still takes mind to do that. Whether as one big mind or many minds interconnecting and interacting with each other. Yes we're still integrating with each other just as we did when we had only developed as far as protons and neutrons etc. We all came from one god source, but we never actually separated, we just grew and stayed connected by one form of energy or another.

I've played about with energy. My friend Josie and I would meet up each week at the same time in the same room just to connect to higher energies. Because of our commitment, the energy that built up was so strong that we could sense the change the moment we walked in the room. The pressure seemed lighter and more uplifting, which gave an immediate calming feeling. I remember using a pendulum to ask questions with. Each pendulum moves its own way due to its own vibration, so it is always a good idea to ask which way is yes and which way is no. If you just happen to pick up a pendulum and start asking questions you may not get much from it. But if you give it time and use regularly, the energies can build up quite strong. The only real way to know that this works, is to do it yourself. Watching others can leave room for doubt, due to the fact that it is not easy to keep your hand completely steady. This one time I remember expecting one answer when I got a totally different answer. The pendulum swung in completely the opposite direction to which I had expected it to. Not only that but it swung with great force and I knew then that other energies were controlling the pendulum rather than my own mind. On most other occasions I seemed to know the answer that I was going to receive. As all minds are connected. We either pick up on the information that is right for us at the time or spirit / the universe can interconnect their energy to influence our part of the energy. Of course, we are in control of our part and we can only be influenced if our own higher mind chooses.

Further in we would practice relaxing our vision, in order to see the colours in our auras. This is more easily done against a plain soft neutral coloured background, with soft lighting I remember training in crystal therapy surrounded by white walls and bright white light. Because we were working in a relaxed state I could see auras all over the place and each day I would leave totally drained with a terrible headache. However white is great for reflecting colours. When the eyes are focused on one point for a length of time preferably without blinking. The vision relaxes and colour can be seen around the other person's body. It was at this time during a day on the crystal therapy course, when I first experienced past regression. This helped me immensely, as since then I have constantly travelled back in time during this lifetime. It has helped to release childhood traumas as part of my healing process. I also used hypnotherapy to help with this. Having someone in the profession to talk you through and past obstacles is very helpful.

Later on we would take it in turns relaxing our bodies and allowing other energies to enter our bodily space. It was amazing to be able to feel the different personalities within our bodies. One minute I would be slouching in my chair, feeling totally bloated in my stomach as though I had a little pot belly. The next I would be sat upright with a stern look upon my face. Josie would sit opposite and describe what she could see with her relaxed vision. We would then swap and she would allow the different energies within herself, whist I tried to describe what I could see. I have to say I wasn't very good at focusing, but one thing totally shocked and amazed me. As I was continually focusing trying to see someone else within Josie and not having much success at all. All of a sudden an old lady just jumped out at me, as if to give one big effort for me to see her. Well I nearly fell off my chair with shock and then just burst out laughing. It's probably one of the most amazing things that I've experienced.

We went on to learn about and experience colour in a little more depth. During this time we found that colour was not just a pretty thing to look at, but that there was much more to it. As we have said the white light runs into our bodies, our body uses the different vibrational colours within. As we take on the stresses of life, these colours of energy can become blocked. Causing disease in the parts of the body that they resonate with. There are many energy centers all over the body which flow the energy in and around us, similar to the hearts function with our blood circulation. However as with anything it is much easier, for us to focus on the main ones which have become known as the 7 chakra system.

This consists of our base or root chakra which is red and located at the perineum. This colour nourishes the spinal column and kidneys in the body which is why it assists with boosting energy. Energy connects with our ambition and drive to keep moving forward, so it affects our consistency. This all relates to our earthly physical needs such as finances, career and necessities.

The sacral is found in the area of the naval, lower abdomen. Its orange nourishes the reproductive system, which is why this area is very much affected by our thoughts and feelings concerning emotions and relationships. This is where the root of cravings and addictions seem to start which explains why I'm constantly drawn to wearing my orange top of late. I'm presently trying to release that which is affecting my constant comfort eating. At this moment in time I feel like I am constantly trying to fill a black hole. Now that's going to take forever, so the only way to stop myself is to find the cause of the black hole and release it.

The solar plexus is located just above the navel nourishing the stomach, liver gall bladder and nervous system. This one has been a major hurdle for me coming from a nervous family. I have struggled with depression in the past (which is a breakdown of the nervous system) and just recently had an episode before starting to write. I don't fear it anymore as I have learnt to understand it. I now put all the guilt aside, get help from the doctor as soon as possible and take time out. In fact I basically just slept for a year because my body needed the rest. I explained as much as I could to those around me and if they couldn't understand, it was there problem to deal with not mine. I have to say, because I'd made up my mind to help myself. Everyone else just accepted it. You may notice the solar plexus take on stress, especially if you're watching a thriller or scary movie. Notice a dull pain just below your chest when something makes you jump. That's your solar plexus taking on stress. If this happens it's a good idea to do plenty of deep breathing to release it, before this area becomes blocked with a constant build up. The problem with TV is that we don't use our fight or flight as we would in real life situations, so we don't release the stress taken on board.

The heart chakra is found to have both pink and green. The green resembles healing and balance. While the pink is made up of the red from the base, our lowest vibrational frequency of colour and purple which is the highest frequency of colour which we perceive. A perfect balance for love. From hear these colours can nourish the heart and its circulatory system which travels around the body as a whole. It is affected by our thoughts and emotions to do with love, relationships and people's attachments. It is also where we connect with divine love from god and our higher self. Here we learn forgiveness of oneself and others. This area can become over run with held back tears, or it can become so blocked that we just don't have any feelings or emotions for anyone or anything. To open up this area again, we need to find something that was very dear to us and focus on bringing the love back for that one thing until we can expand on it. Keeping something pink close by can help greatly.

The throat chakra is just where it says, around the throat area. It nourishes the bronchial and vocal apparatus, lungs and alimentary canal. Her thoughts and feelings are taken in the body then transformed into expression. The blue helps provide space from the self to enable inner reflection. This colour was a big favourite of mine, blue clothes, blue rooms, blue jewellery etc. I didn't process thoughts and feelings very well. Instead I held on to grudges and found it difficult to let go. I spoke very little so I didn't release any of the emotions. When I did speak I found difficulty in putting things across in an acceptable way for others. I spoke bluntly and although I never meant harm with my honest speaking It didn't always come across that way. I found myself very bitter deep down and in time that bitterness developed toward myself. I've had constant problems with my neck and jaw. I've come to realise that we can't just think about things and move on. The process is much deeper. The connection between here and the sacral chakra is possibly where I developed an addiction to smoking during my rebellious teenage years.

The third eye situated slightly above the center of the eyebrows. Also known as the brow chakra. The colour of Indigo is drawn here nourishing the lower brain, left eye, and ears nose and nervousness system. I have found the area around my left eye and front part of the head to be the main blockage causing my allergic rhinitis and hay fever. Massaging this area helped release the symptoms. As for the nervousness system. On receiving the truly wonderful gift of reiki, our higher god consciousness makes minor adjustments within the nervous system according to each student. That student will then go on to a cleansing and releasing process. During this experience I opened up to a lot of the closed thinking that I'd had previous. It was like waking up and realising things then allowing them to be released. I suppose it was like a mega reiki treatment. You see reiki and other forms of healing work with pure white light or energy. As this is pure love, we have to release old stubborn habits to make way for the opening of our heart chakra. The more this happens, the more love can flow through. So you see no harm can be done with healing, because it doesn't work without love. The more we love the stronger the healing. The less we love, the less it works. Opening up the third eye chakra works on lifting our vibration to a higher frequency, in order to connect to our higher being. This is where we can access information and where spirit will lower there vibration to meet us half way. This is why we see them in a dream like transparency, rather than solid as they were when they were here.

The crown chakra is mainly the colour of violet, but can also be white or gold. These colours nourish the upper brain and right eye. Here is where we connect to the universe. When I first started to connect, I experienced a very strong tingling sensation right on and around my crown. This chakra is affected by thoughts and feelings relating to god/ the universe/ the divine/ spirituality/religion. This is where we experience knowledge beyond our words or intellect.

These chakras are vortices within our subtle body. They draw in information and send it to those parts in our body where needed. They also send out Information.

This is how we can get a feeling of someone else's emotional state, without having actually interacted with them. We can all hide our emotions in the physical body, but we still show them in our subtle body and that can expand way beyond our physical body. Interconnecting with others.

Finding out that our body draws in information vier its vortices, helps me understand how precious stones and rocks formed in the earth can hold information. They are part of the earth which has a polar vortex surrounding both of the poles. It also forms more vortices in the way of such things like whirlpool and tornadoes etc. it was once thought that we were part of a vortex, however as scientists find out more about our solar system ideas change. Who's to say we are not part of a bigger vortex that we cannot yet see. This is why a certain crystal rock holds certain information depending on its colour. That colour vibration then resonates with our chakras (or vortices) to transmit information. This is why the closer we place a crystal to the same coloured chakra, the more help, information and healing we can gain from it. The same can be said for essential oils, as these too have a colour or have come from plants containing a colour.

If we go back to the beginning of time. Everything was created with vortices. It's how gravity exists and they're still in our building blocks of life right now.

It was during a colour course that I experienced energy in a completely new and different way than I had before. About 5 of us sat down ready for a meditation. The sun was shining and I felt very comfy on the end of a cosy sofa. I totally relaxed into it. All of a sudden I startled myself. I had relaxed so much that I just rose out of my body. What suddenly made me aware was that I had passed through the door, which had been left open at the side of the sofa. I say passed, but it felt as though I had half passed through and half bumped into it. A very strange feeling to say the least. I now wish I'd stayed a little longer to experience it, but I realised that I'd gone so deep that if I didn't start bringing myself round straight away then I wouldn't be back in time for the next part of the teaching. I got straight back into my body and started to ground myself. Sure enough I was the last one to open my eyes but made it back into the physical just in time. Vibrating at such a high frequency that I could actually pass through something solid was an amazing experience for me, and something I'll never forget. This wasn't the only time I'd lifted out of my body. I did it a couple of other times during my sleep. Of course at these times it's hard to know if it's just a dream. I never went far, just around the bedroom in fact. On one occasion I got quite confused. My ex-husband half asleep at this time. On seeing my spirit walking around the bedroom, thought he was seeing a ghost. Which I suppose he was, only the ghost was me. On being startled by what he saw, he grabbed my arm next to him and started to shake me awake telling me there was a ghost in the room with us. The moment he touched my physical body my attention took me straight back into it. The funny thing was that I went to lift my head up to answer him and I found that I wasn't fully in my body. I automatically put my head down again until my physical head came with it, leaving me quite confused as to what had just happened.

Everything I learnt through this period of my life gave me a great understanding of the energy that flows through our bodies and how blockages occur causing our everyday aches and pains. In my twenties it would take me a fare few minutes to straighten up after leaning over the bath to bathe the children. In the evening as I grew tired I would struggle to sit still comfortably in a chair. It made me wonder how much I would struggle in old age, if I was like this so early on in life. I learned to use my mind and imagination to flow the energy around my body again, releasing blockages which were sometimes hard to shift. I figured by this time as it had taken me thirty plus years to get into this state, it was going to take a pretty long time to get back to a pure state of health. Never the less that was not going to stop me. The gift of Reiki has certainly pushed me forward. There are many types out their now due to change and advancement. I certainly recommend this to anyone who is thinking about it. If it's on your mind, you're ready. No harm can come of this wonderful gift, it is completely natural. It is an insight, an awakening to the self and our capabilities which boosts our own ability to selfheal.

From here I developed new ways of healing myself. If I get myself comfy and lie still I can focus on all the pains within my body. On doing this I will allow my attention to focus on the strongest pain. As I focus on the pain and feel it completely, I can sometimes follow it through my body. You see what happens is on not wanting to move forward in life due to fear, we may stub a toe for instance. That stress from that experience along with all the others piled on top can have a knock on effect. As this happens they build up layer upon layer causing more stressful situations, to add even more stress to the body. The pressure from the blocked energy then builds in the body, to cause pain in one part of the body. This then causes more blockages and has a knock on effect, causing more pain in another part of the body. To release a pain in our head for instance, we may have to travel down the neck and into the back where we tend to store the buildup. That might release aches and pains into the shoulders, where we have been carrying burdens for many years. On releasing from the shoulders we might then get a buildup in the neck, where our outlook on life may be rigid. Our attitudes may then be affecting our throat, sinuses eyes and ears. Are our ears becoming clogged because we don't like what we hear and don't want to listen? Are we seeing things clearly? Is there an over load of emotions that need a release causing colds, hay fever or sinusitis? Do we have trouble speaking out, or letting our mouth run away with us? Before you know it, we are back to that first pain in our head. To release that we need to release all the other stuff. It takes time but is well worth doing. It affects every part of our existence. The more you can release, the more you can notice a difference for the better. Of course using all the other methods of healing at different times, alongside my own healing methods. Has helped greatly as just in life, things move along a little quicker and easier with a little help. I have often used musk oil during self-healing, to increase my awareness to that which I am letting go. I found this to work amazingly well. All you have to do on bringing all these issues to the surface for healing, believe it or not is just breathe. Yes, just deep breathe and let it go. I don't always let go of the whole issue that has been brought to mind. Sometimes I may hold on to a part of it for further processing until I'm ready to let go. As I let go of more and more, I am slowly becoming more aware of my eating habits. I tip back and forth like a set of scales trying to balance as I eat healthy, then fall back into eating the old rubbish again. I'm learning to balance how much and how often I eat, still swinging back and forth. At this point I'm beginning to realise that slowly changing a little at a time without throwing out too many bad habits at once, is going to be the key for me. As much as I would like everything to have happened yesterday, that's not how it works and if I try to heal too quickly without learning the lessons. Then something is going to keep pulling me back until I do. I may not be my old slim healthy self today, but I am losing weight and gaining back my health right now. Even if I can't see it due to the fluctuations.

As I get further on with my healing I have learnt to talk to my body, (sounds daft I know). Whilst receiving help from a hypnotherapist, I found that my own mind would not always take me the way I wanted it to. For example as I walked in my own mind through a wonderfully green pasture, I came across a barbed wire fence. On wanting to pass, I found I couldn't. If I tried to go under, the fence lowered to stop me and if I tried to go over it lifted higher stopping me again. The hypnotherapist told me to ask the fence why it would not let me through. On asking the question, I started to realise that I was talking to my own fear. I explained that I would be safe and that I wouldn't go far. I carried on to explain that I wouldn't be gone long and promised to return safely after just taking a look. As I did this the fence lowered and allowed me to pass. It hooked onto me again trying to pull me back, but with a little more reassurance let me go further on my journey. The reason this has continued to help with my healing process, is that I can now talk to by body and ask why it hurts in certain areas. On understanding the cause, it helps me talk my body into letting go of emotions and the pain caused by them.

After any type of healing it is possible, to feel what's known as crystals in parts of the body. These are the little clicks sometimes heard, or felt as everything is brought to the surface. You will find that the treatment you have received is just the start of the process. Over the next few days whether noticed or not, we go through experiences bringing to light issues that cause the emotions ready to be released. Don't worry if you don't as things like this become more noticeable later on, when enough stuff has been removed for us to be able to see the light so to speak It is important to rest as needed and drink plenty of water to help flush out the toxins. Fun, laughter and exercise also work well at this time I also use yoga to help with the release.

Well as I have already told you about my allergic rhinitis, constantly sneezing at anything that tickled the senses in my nose. Even with the medication I wouldn't leave the house without tissues at the ready. Today I don't take any. No more pills and as for tissues, any I do take seem to be for everyone else. I find it quite funny after all the stick I've had over the years. You know when you get something back that you have done without for years, such as your sense of smell. It's like a little place of heaven. It's like being a child again smelling flowers for the first time.

There are many that have similar experiences to myself. Something's aren't realised and other things just aren't talked about. Let's face it, if it's hard to believe ourselves then who else is going to believe it. The more we hear about these things that happen. The more we are likely to experience them, due to the fact that we are more aware and therefore able to notice them. This is why more and more are coming to light. I've noticed myself, that people are less afraid to talk about their experiences and that people you really wouldn't expect claim to have seen a ghost or two. The more Information we share, the more open to possibilities we become. The more we experience, the more information we have access to and the faster we grow. The more we learn the less we fear. There really is nothing to be afraid of.

MIRRORED IMAGES

Isn't it amazing to think that we can create our own world and we have the power within us to get to where we want to be in life? We are like a whole universe crammed into a human body. Mini universes within a universe. Every part of us dependent on each other to function properly, keeping our state fit, healthy and in working order. Just like our world depends on every other part of the universe, functioning just the way it does. The same elements that create the universe, create us and our very existence. We are like magnets attracting everything to us, without even stopping to realise our thoughts that pass through our heads. In some cases we don't even know why life has taken us to where it has. We are evolving rapidly, children can pick up the latest technology with a click of a finger.

Meanwhile I'm still trying to figure out my smart phone, not to mention Facebook, Twitter and everything else out there that has come into being.

More people have a part to play in their creation than we realise. The original thought may not be as original as we first think. Given that all our thoughts are connected. They go out into the universe, adding together with other thoughts and spurring on the process triggering even more thoughts. It only takes one person to pick up on those thoughts and put them into action. Then hey presto! More people than we realised, unknowingly actually helped create it. Think about it, how many of us actually have ideas to do things but don't. We may feel they are silly or unrealistic because we are still in the mindset, of feeling unworthy or undeserving of what we can actually achieve and have. So we leave it to someone else to get a similar idea and then years later we say to ourselves, 1 thought about doing that too. Just for a moment we get a feeling of excitement confirming that we are as clever as the next person. All any of us have to do to be alike, is to follow our ideas through to the end. Many of us are in the mind set of focusing on situations in life that go wrong or badly. We often let ourselves listen to other people, rather than listening to ourselves. We can go anywhere and do absolutely anything that we desire in life. We just have to believe in ourselves, knowing that we are as good and as equal as every other living soul out there.

I am not religious nor am I a scientific expert, although I use them to get me to where i want to be. I do not follow a religion or keep myself up to date on the latest scientific evidence, I do believe in them all as a whole. What I believe is that each of them are simply trying to get the same message across, which is basically love and faith just like in the law of attraction.

Not all of us can get our heads around all the scientific vocabulary. It is not familiar to us, but when brought into reality with stories and different teachings we start to understand more. How are we expected to understand fully, what and who we really are? When from a young age we go to school learning in one lesson that we go to, about how gods and goddesses create the world. Then the next one we go to, teaches about molecules, atoms and the big bang. Even then we are pushed and pulled into different directions of thinking. We have to learn although we don't fully understand. We then we get marked and tested to see if we are classed as clever. From a young age we are tested and categorised into sets on learning subjects, that we don't even know when we will use in our lives.

We take with us a sense of feeling clever or not so clever into our later years and go through life with a feeling of a need to prove ourselves. Just like when we pass our driving test, but never really learn to drive until we are behind the wheel in total control of the car for ourselves.

My niece and I have come to the same conclusions in life, but have both gone about it in completely different ways. As I'm sure that one day all religions and scientists alike will hit a point where they have the same answers. There will be no more need for wars or violence, greed or power over what or who is right and wrong. A stage when all are balanced, bringing the whole world back into balance. One thing we have had to do in order to get our answers, is to completely understand ourselves and that means we have had to learn to lovingly accept every aspect of ourselves. Without coming to this understanding, we would not be where we are now. From my point it has been extremely hard at times, amazing and fun all at the same time.

I am a person who has to find answers for myself. People come into my life to guide me or steer me in the right direction, but I always go my own way according to how I feel about a situation. I came to a point in my life where I knew exactly what I wanted, with both my career and personal relationships. Then bang, it was as though I'd hit a brick wall and didn't know which way to turn. This was because I was very stubborn in my ways and had built up so many protection barriers in my head. It was as though that little voice inside myself was trying to tell me right. (Sue) if you want everything you desire to come into fruition, then those stubborn walls you have built up are going to have to come down'. It has been a feeling of vulnerability and being open to everything as I've let things go. It's a little like going back to being a child again, being more open and vulnerable. Only this time with lessons learnt and the ability to stay more in balance. Because I had become so open, I could see myself in every single person that I came across and I could love everyone without getting emotionally attached. It's a little like when you've lost someone close and you start to notice people that look like, or remind you of them. Or meeting someone new and feeling like you already know them. I had to be careful at this point, as not all of us have learnt to follow the good inside of us. I had to be quick to spot the warning signals, from that which I had already learnt in life. I had learnt to be strong enough to let go of people and situations that weren't right for me, following my instinct rather than my head. In the past I have always seen the good in everyone, to the extreme of giving to everyone. Continuing to help them by taking on their strains and struggles, completely forgetting about myself. Once my protection barriers had gone I would still come across similar situations, but I had started to notice when I needed to put myself first. I have found that life goes around in circles, until we can finally break free from our comfort zones and live life to its fullest.

As a child I had no fear and was always willing to try anything that was put before me, I would go up on stage at the drop of a hat. Ride a motorbike without knowing how to stop.

It's almost as though when we are children we have that inner strength and as we get older, fear in life seems to take over. We don't do what we want to do and addictions of any kind fill in that void from where something is missing. Once the fear barriers are broken in adulthood, that inner strength comes back. This is where the saying 'listen to your inner child' comes in. Remove all the layers and we are still that child who can do, achieve and accomplish. Just a little older with a number for our age and the wisdom gained from the school of life. Once the fear has gone and we have surrendered to life's flow, without letting life control our emotions. We have the strength and wisdom to carry on evolving. Who knows what we can manifest into being.

During my life I have struggled with unhappy relationships. I have experienced both mental and physical abuse. Although I struggled as a teenager with different addictions such as smoking and a little later on drinking. I managed to turn my life around, to developing a more positive outcome. I have had to bring myself to a point of understanding. Analysing the whole person and situations that I have come across. Due to these suppressed feelings on top of other emotions growing up. By the time I had children I suffered with post-natal depression. I also started to develop arthritis. Every day things such as brushing and mopping a floor or bathing the kids, became very painful activities. It has certainly held me back in my career, causing me to bounce from one career to another. Of course I do believe that it is possible to cure myself. But I make no mistake in realising that it has taken years of unreleased stress and anxiety to get me to this sorry state. It will take a bit more to get me to a balanced state of health again, especially when my body still takes on stress of different kinds on a daily basis.

Astrology has been a massive part in my life. I find it fascinating to think that people have studied and worked out our star/ zodiac signs, categorising every month and birth date by the planets. Many think this is all nonsense, but everything in this universe has a part to play. Everything causes an effect however big or small. Everything that moves causes a push or pull effect. Even the moon as far away as it is manages to push and pull on our emotions and we certainly have plenty of them. It is often said that there is no love like your first love! I feel that although this is the norm. I feel it is possible to have those feelings again that we felt for our first love. Our problem is that we carry our hurt and pain with us into the next relationship that we have and so on. How many times do we see or know of people who go from one bad relationship to the next. How many of us are really truly happy, right up to the end. The same as addictions, we use drama and arguments to fill in that space in our lives. Then we hit old age and it's as if we have learnt to live with our partner. We learn to accept them the way they are, letting them get on with being themselves. We start to mellow with age, but wouldn't it be amazing if we could learn to love ourselves unconditionally from the start of life and keep on doing so without the negative impact that life has on us. By doing this we would be more likely to accept others without judgment. You see our relationships suffer because the more harshly we judge ourselves expecting perfection, the more we see our imperfections mirrored in the people around us.

Even with astrology we are looking at our personalities and yet if we were to stop and realise that everything out there has an effect on our personalities, interfering with our emotions causing our mood swings. Surely we would realise that if we are not in full control of ourselves, how can we expect others to be in full control of their selves. Of course if we are at an all-time low in our life, then we attract people of that same vibrational frequency. So if you want more positive happier people in your life. You better pick yourself up, dust yourself off and get your mindset back on track. Positive happy people don't want to stick around people with low vibes or they will find themselves feeling the same way.

We all live by the law of attraction whether we know it or not, but how many of us really understand it. I read books on the subject but on their own that wasn't enough to change my life. It took an awful lot of brainwashing and reprogramming to really get myself to a place where I could see clearly the changes it could make in my life. Using the law of attraction in a positive loving way, brought me back to myself as a child. Less judgement and more excitement. A child that lives for the day and in the moment. I have heard it said that the law of attraction only brings greed. I beg to differ as the law of attraction only brings to us that which we are.

I have always analysed everything in front of me and have often despised myself. It has been such a habit that I have just wished I had a switch to turn my brain off for a while just to rest. However that is something I must learn to balance. I have struggled being around people constantly needing alone time. Wanting things done perfect and easily angered or upset if someone interfered.

I couldn't understand why it was so difficult for me to be around others. I am a person who can speak quite bluntly, with never any harm meant. However under the influence of alcohol I would come across a little too blunt sometimes causing offence. Even if I hadn't caused offence I would come away worrying constantly in case I had. Judging myself more harshly than ever because I hadn't been perfect. Over time I've realised that suppressing my fear of being myself and staying quiet for fear of saying the wrong thing. Has actually held me back from enjoying others company. As I became more balanced I realised that I could be in the company of others without feeling like I had to be the perfect social one. I could actually be in someone's company without the need to make constant conversation. I finally didn't have to be the one to entertain others or make sure everyone else had a perfect time in my company. I finally realised that the social anxiety that I felt was on everyone's shoulders, not just mine. At last I could stop taking responsibility for everyone else. I was finding my flow. You see if we push out of life's flow, things happen to push us back into place. I was trying too hard instead of relaxing and enjoying the flow that life had to offer.

Sometimes in life we don't even know how we feel in certain situations. More often than not we only think we know. We get addicted to substances to try and make things go away, or stop ourselves from facing up to and thinking about them. One negative thing that we do leads to another and so on. From one glass of wine each night to the odd cigarette and before we know it were also eating unhealthily. We think we enjoy it but before we know it, it stops being something we love doing and becomes a habit we can't break. If we were so happy and balanced, we wouldn't want to do this to ourselves. We wouldn't want to wreck our vehicle that carries us around, getting us from A to B in our lives. We do this because we are scared to face ourselves. We are afraid that if we take away something that is filling in for our hurt and upset. Then we will have to face the very thing that caused us to turn to these habits in the first place. It doesn't stop there. When we cut out that wine, or we quit smoking those cigarettes. We think it is the current situation that makes us feel low and at a loss with ourself. We then point the blame at anyone who is involved. Of course if we were able to remove that person from the situation. That hole and those same feelings would still be there. When we feel a very strong emotion within us. We have to really feel it and understand where it came from in the very beginning. We need to listen to our bodies more, to know and understand how to put our feelings into a balanced state. More often than not, our painful emotions have stemmed from something that happened in our childhood. Once we know where these feelings first started and the root cause. We can then start to heal. Once we can forgive ourselves and admit where we are going wrong. We instantly forgive others who are involved. This is because we come to an understanding, as to why they acted in the way they did at the time. We face our fears and are free to move forward in life.

Sometimes when we are filling in for any kind of addiction, our bodies give us warning signals. We may get a slight ache, pain or even illness. If we ignore these signals, they could eventually turn into something much worse having devastating effects.

Whilst healing my body, I have had to change my diet. This has been trial and error. By listening to my body, I have been able to find the right foods for myself as an individual. We can all listen to the advice from others and information that we read, but I do believe that we should ultimately do that which we feel is right for ourselves. As we have all taken on different stresses in life, we therefore trigger different parts of our bodies to suffer. I also used self-help information from books and the Internet. I used everything that I already knew, along with new advice to try to balance my body a little more. I do believe that we should never let anyone try to tell us what is exactly right for us as individuals. We all are ready to make different changes at different times in our lives. Of course our bodies need water, vitamins and minerals. Just like the earth and all other living things. The amount we need may be different for each individual, as our lives are different and so is the state of our health. Everything is calculated to an average, so when we go into our local supermarket. We are putting our trust in others. We look at labels reading 'sugar free', believing that it is the healthier option. Many fail to read the tiny print with all the ingredients and those that do, don't always understand them. We fail to realise that half the products contain toxins, poisonous to the body. Those small amounts of safe ingredients have now added with others to become a possible harmful amount. Sugar is taken out and replaced with products such as aspartame. Why is this allowed? Because it is calculated on an average so much of this, the body can take and clear away. If we take too much of this we can end up with life threatening diseases, but it is never proven where it comes from when the illness arrives. It is always just a diagnosis of multiple sclerosis or cancer etc. The 'sugar free' label profits. We all think we are eating healthier. A quick way to maybe shed a few pounds. The only way this will stop is when everyone realises and stops buying these products. If the product doesn't sell, there will be no reason to keep making it. It all comes down to making money and greed again.

Our body has a natural PH balance which is slightly alkaline. The more alkaline our diet, the healthier we are. Our food plays a major part in balancing our mind and body. I am not a nutritionist so I can only give you the information from that which I have experienced. I have certainly noticed a big difference in the way I feel since adding more alkaline foods and removing the more acidic foods from my diet. It is proven that from our dict we can prevent and in some cases cure any disease or illness that we have. We should never give up hope if we are diagnosed with anything named incurable.

Finally, last but by no means least. My family have been one of the most important things in helping me heal, let's face it it's hard living with people day in day out. We all have arguments or disagreements. We wouldn't be learning how to get in balance if we just floated through life. I am fortunate to have a family who I love very much, but living with people. All with different personas, is hard work. In the past years I would blame it on their star signs, all having different ones made it a good excuse. Now I have learnt to accept everyone for exactly the way they are and that is because I have accepted myself. I had gone through life analysing everyone, so it was time to analyse myself. Every time I got frustrated, angry, nervous or upset. I started to notice where I had seen those similar characteristics in others. I noticed my over sensitivity in my mum. My dominant aggressive side in my dad and so on. For the first time in my life I felt I had forgiven, not only people I allowed to get on my nerves and upset me. I forgave myself for every mistake I had made towards myself and others. I was grateful for every person being just the way they were and I feel very fortunate. If I didn't have such strong personas in my family, it would have taken a lot longer for me to work out who I really am and why I am the way I am.

Look to the people in your life and start to learn a little about yourself. It's fun, interesting and can help you grow immensely.

I'M AWAKE

As we sit and discuss the topic of how we came into being, leaving us constantly in deep thought of how the universe came to be. How matter and ant-matter (positive and negative) collided in space forming life. So how does this form life? Both matter and anti-matter are equal forces. When they come together they annihilate each other, turning into pure energy. For some unknown reason, it would seem that for every billion particles of anti-matter there are a billion and one particles of matter. Well it may not seem a lot but that one particle left over from each collision, created the whole universe!

It is not yet known why there is more matter on earth and only traces of anti-matter. It seems to be that if matter and anti-matter cancel each other out and turn into pure energy then that pure energy has to go somewhere. The matter that was left over had nothing else to cancel itself out, therefore creating the solidity of the whole solar system. We do believe that the energy is inside of all living things. Put like this, matter + anti-matter = energy. So energy + matter = living things.

This is the same way two peoples worlds collide, (male/female). Our paths cross, we fall in 'love' and we reproduce creating life and helping evolution along its way. Now look at it like this. (Matter / positive / female) and (anti-matter/negative / male). Both are opposites but whether we are male or female on the outside, we have both energies on the Inside. Living in the society we do today we learn and are programmed to play the role of male and female. As a child everything is magical and exciting but the male gender are given toys such as cars, work trucks etc. As they get older they feel they should keep their emotions to themselves, as they are meant to be the strong protectors and are afraid to show their feelings in case they are scrutinised for not being 'manly'. The female gender. The complete opposite, are given dolls from a young age. They are taught to nurture and care for others often before they can even learn how to care for themselves. Then boy meets girl and the two without even realising, are dependent on each other. The female needs someone to look after and protect her. The male needs someone to feel emotions for him and nurture him.

So we haven't learnt to use and balance the energy, as we have programmed ourselves to play the male or female roles. The same way we haven't learnt to balance our thought process to use successfully with the law of attraction.

Remember how we said earlier in the book that our brain is like a computer. We are the drivers of our vehicles and the keyboard to our Information source. Sometimes we fail to realise that no matter whether we are a male or female, we are all equal. We just need to wake up and realise how powerful we are in a balanced state. Powerful meaning that we can manifest our desires, love ourselves and others unconditionally. As we realise that although we all have different personas, we are all one and the same. You may have heard spiritualists mention the kundalini awakening, some may say waking up or seeing the light. It doesn't really matter what we call it, religions and scientists may call it totally different names, only with the same meaning. The kundalini awakening is when one gender awakens to the dormant energy inside their selves. Putting this into clearer perspective, the female awakens to the masculine energy that has been lying dormant and the male awakens to the female energy that has been dormant When one wakes up the opposing energy, it is possible that we could have a higher energy to when this was lying dormant. Learning how to use this energy, like everything in life has to have a balance.

Have you ever heard the saying 'the dark of the soul' it is just before you have your 'ah' moment and awaken to this divine energy. We see it a little like this, every human being has feelings. Some may feel more towards love and happiness, others more towards fear and sadness. No matter what we feel more of, we all know of these feelings. Of course a major event in our lives. Such as amazement, abundance or bereavement and grief can shake us up a little to push us along our way, to believe in something more than the everyday mundane world that we live in as people. We need to know what sadness is, to know what happiness is.

We need to feel fear to know what love is, what right from wrong is and so on. If we don't feel these feelings, how will we ever learn to balance our emotions and find our peace? If we cannot love ourselves the good the bad and the ugly, then we cannot show our love to others. Loving ourselves is not just about looking in the mirror and saying yes I love myself, it's a great feeling of forgiving ourselves of any mistakes we have made. Being grateful for everything we have such as eyes to see, ears to hear, a nose to smell, a tongue to taste, hands to touch and feel. To love ourselves is to understand our own emotions and know who we are as a person. When we completely love ourselves we can love our partner, family and friends, no matter what their faults. If we unconditionally love a person, we would not want them to change. We would accept the good, bad and ugly in them as with ourselves. We would want them to just be them. Of course we're not saying we should let people walk all over us, or stay in an abusive relationship. We're simply saying that we should not expect too much. We should be whole and happy enough to not put each other down, or tell the other person what they should or shouldn't be doing. We cannot make a person love us the way we desire to be loved, nor can we change someone into the person we dream of. We can only change ourselves. To who we are at the core of our being to who we are at our happiest. As we change ourselves the other person will either mirror back to us who they really are at their best, or naturally fall away from us in a mutual agreement. If we are still not happy in someone else's company, then we should be able to give an honest explanation and walk away. When we are completely happy in our own skin, we want nothing more than for ourselves and the other person to be happy.

It seems to be, that we are all on a journey of the self. When we say this we do not mean in a selfish manner. Selfish would mean to be a person who wants power, thinking of their selves in a higher position than others. Every single race, religion, male and female on the planet are equal and the same. So you may say, well that person is a billionaire and I am poor. The sweet fact is that we are all skin, bones and soul. In this world if we want something we have to go out and get it, if we want to be heard we have to speak up. We have to love and believe in ourselves. Knowing that we can do anything that we want in life and we are equal to others. Yes money is freedom, but money is also just paper and brass. Materialistic things are fabulous things that we have created, but everything has started from an idea. Imagine if you could take yourself back in time, you have no clothes and no home. Your sensory system would still tell you when you are too hot, cold or need food. So you would automatically listen to your intuition and thoughts. Eventually you would find food and have an idea for warmth and shelter. Today everything is built and done for us. Jobs on the market, in stores, towns and cities, studies for school. Options to take and decisions to be made. We don't need to listen to our intuition for survival any more, as we don't have the constant need to look out for predators. So the mind takes over. We are lead to believe that we should be in the highest paid jobs that we can get, we don't follow our gut instinct we follow money. When we follow our instinct, we follow our individual passions and talents. The rewards then come to us. The things we need do not always have to come in the form of money, as this is only a means of exchange. We are happy at what we have achieved and keep achieving. The people attracted into our lives are similar to us and on the same wave length. So when we follow money and high paid jobs, the money starts to take over. We try to get higher positions for the money, not the passion. If we are not careful money and materialistic goods can start to take over our lives. We can become workaholics, forgetting about our own happiness and push loved ones away. This is because the money and business come first, even before ourselves. The people attracted into our lives are of money minded and before we know it, it's hard to know who we can trust in the world. Think about it, we work hard for the money to enjoy life. We can then sometimes hold onto the money as a security blanket out of fear, forgetting the real value of it Again it's all about balance, balancing your security and enjoyment.

Whoever we attract into our lives are mirroring part of us, every person that we meet is bringing us closer to the self. If we can't see or deny the fact, then we need to look closer. This is how we can start to learn the balance of the energy inside us. The easiest way to start is to look closest to home, our parents, brothers, sisters, partners and children. The things we love about the people around us are what we should give ourselves credit for, as somewhere in our lives we will be doing the same. The things that really irritate us or annoy us in a person, are keys to help us understand that which we can change in ourselves. If we are noticing things in others. Then we must be repeating them ourselves, however small. Sometimes as people we find it hard to take responsibility for our own actions. It is far easier to point the blame at someone else, than to see where we ourselves are going wrong. The easiest way to see things from a clear perspective, is to completely take ourselves out of a harsh situation. It is then easier to see the bigger picture of how things have happened and can be put right. If we find this hard to do we can always treat ourselves, how we would treat our best friend or a loved one. The trick is to always follow that good voice inside ourselves and we can't go far wrong.

Very often in life we can get taken advantage of. This can sap our energy if we allow it. Our failure is when we as a kind giving person, try to help as much as we can until we have nothing left to give. This is known as passive behaviour. We need to know when to say enough is enough and to give ourselves the same respect that we give to others. No matter how hard we try, we cannot help someone who doesn't want to be helped. We can't always help until the time comes, when they are ready. If we stay in a situation where someone is draining us, then we will only cause ourselves harm. We often find especially with children, that the more passive of people will attract the more aggressive or strong willed. As the two will balance each other out. As the more passive child grows and learns, there is a bit of push and pull. If the more dominant of the two hasn't become less dominant to be in line with the more passive child, then arguments erupt until they part company. The two will move on to find more balanced friendships. This is why fewer people stay together throughout their whole lives. We are evolving faster and all at different paces. Because we are not in the flow of life as we should be some will speed ahead learning life's lessons in fast spurts. Then some will slow down while others catch up and so on. If we stay in and spend too much time together in these relationships that aren't really working for us, we end up with pent up feelings of emotions. All these bad feelings trapped inside ourselves, will attract more of the same into our lives.

Often, we can sometimes be too quick to judge others. Who has the right to say what should be normal in the world. Isn't it unique and fantastic to be able to stand on our own two feet? To be proud of who we are and what we are so lucky to see in others. When we judge other people too quickly or even at all, then we clearly have our own insecurities that need to be dealt with. Take bullying with children for example. As adults it is sometimes possible to see where it is all going wrong as we are on the outside looking in and yet we still make the same mistakes ourselves. As we grow and learn the habits we formed may become more subtle. However for those of us who don't learn so easy from our mistakes, we get worse. Then there are of course those of us who just get better at covering things up. So if you still have complicated relationships with people and let's face it we all do from time to time. If you want things to change, it's time to ask yourself why you are attracting such relationships. Those of us who have problematic relationships and love drama, can sometimes find the quieter more well behaved people unappealing. We will only find these people an attraction as we change for the better ourselves, as we become less hooked on drama. From a young age we can become fearful of being left on our own, without friends and support. Some will take control by manipulating others into being friends or liking them. The trouble with this is that it becomes hard work and something that must be constantly worked at. It takes a strong person to not let their emotions get the better of them, causing them to behave in such a manner where they must always have control. That is why those who get bullied and are seen to be weak, are usually much stronger. They have an inner strength that does not have to be flaunted in their character. This is all down to balance again. From inside us we should be kind without being too soft and on the surface we should show a firmness, without being aggressive or even passive aggressive. When you look at how many people a bully can manipulate into being a part of their gang. Or even adults who draw people together in order to harm others, as like attracts like. It just goes to show how many of us are actually very fearful. Those who refuse to join are actually facing their fears by refusing to become a part of what they know to be wrong, knowing that there may be consequences. Sometimes in life a good person will attract negative behaviour to them. This does not have to be an intimate relationship, it can be in the form of friendship or a workmate etc. This happens when we give to everyone and have a positive attitude with everyone around us, but leave ourselves out of the equation. The only way that we will ever stop any of this from happening is if we heal ourselves from any stress and trauma that we have taken on in our lifetime. The sad thing is that a lot of the healing methods are not available to children. Surely it is better to heal ourselves from a young age as we take on stress, than let it build up layer upon layer until it is harder to shift. However there has been a shift in consciousness and many are now waking up to the reality that holistic therapies do work. People are starting to realise that medicine although it can help, it can cause side effects or just mask over the problem. With immediate effect they can cure pain but not necessarily heal the condition. I remember a time when I started to learn reiki, how I was laughed at and told so many times it was a load of rubbish. It is now practiced in hospitals and my own doctors encourage me to keep working on myself with it. The great thing about this is that more and more healing methods are becoming encouraged and available to the young such as baby massage.

Of course looking back over what we have said. We are all the same. The strength or weakness is only noticed differently to others when it is out of balance. We have to be weaker in one way in order to be stronger in another way.

Something always has to give. We are only truly at our strongest when every part of our being is balanced.

Everything in life has to have a balance whether it's diet, health, relationships, careers or even something else. If one thing is out of balance, it can tip everything out. We can end up fighting with ourselves, our angel on one shoulder arguing with our devil on the other shoulder. This is the polarised energy that we hold within us. Often when this is out of balance, we need other people's opinions to steer us in the right direction. Listening to other people's opinions is great, but what we have to realise is that not all of us have the same experiences in life. We are not all in a happy balanced state. We can only help each other with that which we have learnt and experienced ourselves.

How do we spot this good voice and bad voice within ourselves? Some times when we hit a low point in life. We do the complete opposite of that, which we know deep down to be the right thing. It is important to remember that we all make mistakes. However we can all learn from any situation. When a similar situation comes back around to us. We tend to ask the question "why me?" Instead we should be asking 'why has this happened? We should be looking for the reason behind the situation. Sometimes we can't find the answers straight away, but if we keep our faith and have patience. The answers will come.

Whatever we give out in life attracts more of the same frequency. It always returns to the source of where it came from. Because this happens. We will only attract either the good that we give out, or the bad that we need to learn from. If we don't like what we are receiving. Then we need to stop giving it out, as we are actually giving it to ourselves.

We see god as a separate being that we can blame for things going wrong. What we are doing is using god as a scapegoat for our own doing. We do not want to take the blame or responsibility ourselves, so we look to something else. We now fail to see that our own higher mind is the godly part of ourselves that connects to all godly parts of all others. That part of our inner truth does not judge us. We are the only ones that pass judgement on ourselves. When we stop judging ourselves, we realise that we never had the right to judge others. When we are capable of connecting to the bigger source, we start to see the whole universe as one.

During meditation when we detach from our physical bodies, we are capable of loving absolutely any one and anything. This is because we can see past there outer being with all their protective walls and see them for their inner beauty. The true soul of pure love, without walls of protective behaviour built up through stress, pain and suffering.

When we reach a stage of enlightenment, the chattering in our minds quieten. Through the silence, we become at one with ourselves. The energies that we hold within are no longer contradicting each other. We are now able to realise that we are the god of our self. We live by the law of attraction creating and planning our lives. Learning to trust in the unknown, that we are going in the right direction. Nothing and no one can pull us from our path. We become at one with our mind, body and soul manifesting every idea, bringing all our dreams into fruition.

Getting to this stage in our lives is certainly challenging. Even when we feel balanced, we can fall back into old behaviour patterns. It can give us a knock especially if we thought we'd changed this part of ourselves. The difference now is that we can more easily notice when this happens in order to get back on track. What it does is gives ourselves the choice to go back to our old way of thinking or we have the choice to stick with the new program that we have given ourselves. We must always put ourselves first and realise our own worth. Even though it is sometimes difficult, we should talk to ourselves as someone we love.

When we hold grudges and ill feeling we create it, not only in our lives but in our bodies. We attract in others that which we hold within, or behaviour we have ourselves. We do this so that which we attract, can teach us what is favourable and what isn't. We are shown our own behaviour from another's perspective. When we learn to forgive ourselves we learn to forgive others and vice versa. As we learn to accept and forgive others, we learn to face ourselves. When we are not balanced we show signs of both positive and negative behaviour. Presenting ourselves as good and bad. Not everyone in life is going to like us. We cannot change people nor can we make them want to be in our company. We can only change ourselves and keep growing. We always have a choice.

So as we evolve we all try to balance ourselves and live according to our own guidance. It's all about shedding the ego. The hard way is always the right way in the sense that it is easy to fall back on negative behaviour patterns, or the things that have once comforted us when things have gone wrong in our lives. It's harder to stay focused on the positive we all too often worry too much about what others think. What we should realise is that if one person judges another they themselves are not perfectly balanced to be perfectly balanced would mean to be non-judgmental and to see a person through the eyes of god. In other words god does not pass judgment. Therefore no one has the right to judge another.

My friend and I went to the pub for catch up. He ordered a glass of wine in a pint glass. I said to him "why would you not just get a wine glass". "Because it's not very manly", he replied. My thoughts were 'how silly, you should never let things like that bother you'. A few weeks later in a restaurant I found myself not ordering a pint of Guinness which was the drink I really wanted, due to it not looking very classy or ladylike. I did not listen to my feelings of which drink was best for me. Instead I went for red wine, knowing full well that it would not react kindly with my skin and body the next morning. I was shown in my friend what I needed to change in myself, before the situation occurred. On failing to learn the lesson, I went on to learn the hard way. When we can't understand a certain part of someone, it most definitely lies within us.

This behaviour comes from the ego. Being scared of what others think, because we are too hard on ourselves. Feeling a need to impress others around us. The ego will only get us so far In life and there will come a point where it has to go, if we are to live a happy balanced life. It is our choice to live in fear with pent up feelings and emotions that we cannot understand. Just as it is our choice to go through life feeling light and sure of love and happiness.

AUTHORITY

Authority started with all good intentions, so we are led to believe. Can this be possible if authority is a way of control, stemming from power? If the people in power were controlling the whole population with all good intention, then surely the world would be a beautiful, wonderful, happy place to live. Even way back in time through the history books of the past. People were enslaved and beaten to force them to create amazing monuments and buildings for the rich and wealthy or the powerful and royalty. Tipping the balance the slaves are set free and we are given freedom of speech, choosing who is in charge for our own best interests. Or have we just swapped our shackles for contracts agreeing to the taxes that were once forced upon our ancestors, thinking we are given much in return. As time goes on we now watch as the things we were offered are slowly taken away and used for other things at the choice of others in power rather than ourselves. Wages slowly rise while the cost of living speeds on ahead. Just as the poor start to catch up a little closer to the rich closing the gap between the rich and poor starting to enjoy life. Something will happen to tip the scales widening the gap again. Where one man's wage was once all you had to live on. The woman being at home to take care of the home, her husband and children. Now men and women bring home a wage that many struggle to make ends meet. We are manipulated more and more into speaking out less and less. Things that were once jokes and laughed at are now scrutinised. Look around you take yourself away from the everyday way of life, shut everything out and be you. Think for you. Now if in control from the top is of good intention, do you think we would be able to buy poisonous foods to fuel our sacred bodies? Everything in small print not big enough for the naked eye to see. Just like the contracts we sign to get credit. It all comes down to money.

Let's start at the beginning as children when we leave our parents side to go to school why do we go to school so early in life, is it to leave our parents free to go to work? Or is work a way of keeping our parents busy, so they're too tired to think too much. As children we are put into schools without the knowledge to handle relationships. Shouldn't we have full lessons on relationships, how they affect us and how we can manage them? How important our actions are and what effects they can have on ourselves and others.

Aren't relationships the most used and most important part of life? What should we be learning in schools that would help us in life? On leaving school, we don't seem to have a clue. We go into Jobs earning wages, paying tax and national insurance. Many of us have no idea what this is or what it's for, let alone how it is calculated. Should this not be one of the main lessons taught in mathematics? Should we not be taught the pros and cons of credit and loans? We all at some point are going to want to own our own home, yet we don't know the first thing about mortgages. Do they want us to get into debt, before we've got off the starting block? We are taught so much and have no interest, because we can't make a connection with the real world. We don't learn which jobs we can use these lessons learned in. By the time we realise where we can use the information, we have forgotten most of it. We leave school having learnt English language. Only to find every contract we come across in life, contains a totally alien language to that which we know. It seems that to learn the real stuff. We have to be well up the ladder of society. Already paying mass taxes to be able to afford and buy our information. On top of the tax, that we are already paying for our education.

We're taught very little on these subjects as we go along through school life, in comparison to that which we learn on other subjects. Even in those subjects we don't seem to be taught how to connect the lessons with life. We find ourselves learning the basics without the knowledge behind what we are learning. Is this to keep us from learning too much, in fear that we may grow and learn asking too many, too deep questions. Whose actually pulling whose strings? As children we think our parents are in control and on being passed over to schools, we think the teachers are in control. Think again! The head teachers are controlled by the governing bodies who are controlled by someone higher and the list goes on. Of course we can take this all the way to the prime ministers and presidents with their governments. Are they in control? Do we really have a say on whose elected, or are there even more behind the scenes that we don't know about? If we are getting better at things all the time, then surely our grades should be soaring through the roof. Have we really not got it right yet, or is someone at the top tweaking things to keep us from being too clever? So we leave school categorised and labelling others. Do we change?

A few of us learn to accept everyone, but very few of us compared to the great size of the population. We're adults now, so can people still control us? How is it that we used to survive on one man's wage, yet we have a job to survive on two people's wages now? Surely with the amount of things we make, create and mass produce, we should be feeling richer not poorer. With the amount of banks we have today, can one corrupt bank really lead us into a recession lasting years? Mind you if we come out of this recession too quickly, the people at the top won't have made enough money and before you know it another world war might be on the agenda. The excuse for this has already been planted and believed with the illusive terrorists. Of course there is always more to a story than we first hear about. There are always other things going on behind the scenes, sometimes more than we can comprehend. As we know everything causes an effect and that has a knock on effect. Given time it all comes to light eventually. We wouldn't all be that daft would we? Think about it, we'd have to be too busy to think. We'd have to work to the point of exhaustion, coming home to eat and sleep. Our rest time would have to be monopolised with TV and video games to keep our minds too busy for contemplation. Our conversations would need a different focus. If we're to busy blaming each other over things, we're forgetting about whose really pulling the strings. Surely they wouldn't take all our money and at the same time giving us the choice to give it, believing we are getting something in return. The taxes we pay are given back to us aren't they? We pay tax when we earn money, we pay when we save it and we pay when we spend it or even when we give it away to our friends and families. We even pay it again when we leave this world. That's got to be enough for the things we've received. After all it is us the people who are recycling the rubbish, teaching our children, treating our patients. Why are prescriptions way more expensive than the same products bought over the counter? How could the country provide us with free dental services as often as they did when we paid so much less? We pay more now and our children's dental appointments have been cut down to a yearly visit, in fact many practices have gone private. Few of us question any of this and those who do, don't get proper answers. Problem is we don't know who to ask because we don't know who pulls the strings. Keep changing the faces in public view with a voting system that we believe is fare and we believe we're still in control putting them in the seat ourselves. Throw a few bombs around and we'll agree to another law thinking it is to protect us, when really all it does it put more restrictions on us. We can't even fight back and protect ourselves anymore, because if we do we are breaking the law. By the time an army of our own people come round under ill intent instruction. They are going against their own loving intent, because they are too afraid not too. The rest of us allow them, because we're too afraid to fight back against authority.

Don't worry, if it is true. We're not as suppressed as some countries. It may not be healthy food, but we can still put some on the table. Some countries are so suppressed that they have now turned to stealing from each other, out of desperation to survive. We wouldn't do that yet, would we? Our country loves us and takes care of us. They love everyone, that's why they keep allowing foreigners to move into the country. They couldn't have possibly foreseen the racism that goes on. New religions and places of worship being brought in to show how welcome and accepted they are. They couldn't have possibly seen that the segregation would cause those rifts and riots that go on. Who could have dreamt that any of us would feel imposed upon as people from foreign countries claim our benefits and send our money home to their own countries. And yet we all do it as the world opens up and becomes more accessible. When we only see what is on our own door step we are closed off to the bigger picture. If the world were in a balanced state then we could all come together treating all as our neighbours. Instead we are lead to believe that there is not enough to go around and the poor suffer while the rich get richer. Of course if were too busy fighting amongst each other, we're certainly not going to have time to see the bigger scheme of things and if we're blaming each other we're not going to think to blame anyone else. Only the lowest of the low would have the mind to create such a master manipulation. The lowest of the low aren't at the top of the chain pulling all the strings. They have too much money to want to do anything so cruel, don't they?

Of course if the world were a perfect place, we could all live freely wherever we please. We could love and accept our neighbours whatever creed or colour and you can bet your life that most of us would. Who's to say that left alone things may have slowly balanced themselves out. And yet all the hype in the news just seems to get everyone's backs up as if prolonging the process or tipping it in the opposite direction.

Our opinions are influenced by the media whether we realise it or not. How much of the information that gets through to us is controlled by the unseen powerful in this world. I agree in helping anyone that needs help near or far. But how many of our own will be left to suffer more, because we are busy helping others from afar that should be being helped by their own. It's all about getting the balance right and yet this can be more difficult than we realise. If we learn to help ourselves we can put ourselves in a much better position to help others. Is this all a little too far fetched? Take a look around you. Does it go on in a similar fashion with smaller people in a smaller way? Do you ever see people manipulating others to get their own way? Do you ever see the richer people amongst us ripping off the poorer people because they can? The bigger and richer they get the better they seem to hide it. The more money they have, the more strings they can pull. No matter how much we have, our ego will always drive us forward to wanting more. People in power with a need to control others have built up so many walls and layers of stress, that they are unable to process their own information clearly. This holds them back in their evolution. As their ego is imbalanced they still have a need to want and move forward, so they do this by taking from others.

Have you ever wondered, why all the things that are bad for us haven't been banned? Of course we are all led to believe that they would then go underground. Would this be so bad? Illegal drugs are no more used, than alcohol and cigarettes. If we want to do something so badly, we will always find a way. Isn't it better to keep it out of site and out of mind? Than to have it widely available, tempting others who would not otherwise have come across it or bothered with it by taking some away and keeping others available. We believe that someone is trying to do right by us. In actual fact it is made available every which way. There is always someone new ready to get addicted. As long as we are addicted, high tax margins can be added. Keeping someone in the way they have become accustomed. Pretty comical how we have all these resources, yet we can't find and stop the mass production. Could it be possible, that they want to keep all this as another means of control?

So what comes next.. Chips implanted in our arms maybe? Of course we will agree to this thinking that it is designed for our protection. It will be so expensive that it will be an achievement to be amongst the first to have them. When all the wealthy have them, the rest of us will want to follow suit. Just like the latest fashions. By the time it's a must have, the price will come down and we will all want one. From there it will become available, free and when there are only a few left without it will be compulsory. So then what? Will they hold all our information keeping us safe or will they keep track on us, making sure we are toeing the line? Will it be like the far fetched movies that have not yet come into being? Just like the old far fetched movies with automatic sliding doors, laser guns and video cameras around every corner watching our every move. Will they program the chip to shut us down, if we refuse to do their dirty work for them? Will we be kept enclosed like animals, just like they did to people during the war?

We already know that robots are on the way they will appear in the same way as the latest must have technology. Before we know it we will have a population of robots living alongside us, stronger than the human race with whose mind controlling them? It certainly won't be a balanced mind, if it's got to this stage of control.

The problem is that most of us are striving to be good, so we just don't see all this creeping up on us. We just wouldn't stop to conceive this as possible, because we could never dream up anything near it ourselves.

Life has changed so much over the years, or has it? We used to take pleasure in seeing people punished, or watching people hang and burn at the stakes. We look back over time, believing that those in power were corrupt and out for their own agenda. What makes us believe that things are so different? Do we feel that we have learnt so much? That because things are shown differently to us, we believe corrupt people have changed for the better? Could it be possible, or is it that media is used to convince us otherwise? Do we feel that because we believe that our country gives so much of our money to charity? They have changed their ways and now they are all good people. We watch with pleasure at seeing other people air their problems on TV. We see in the news children being abused, people being shot, raped and stabbed. If ordinary people are doing these things without a care, what makes us think those in power with control over others are so different? How many people do you come across in life that tell lie after lie or bend the truth to suit? So has anything really changed, or do we just do it a little differently?

It's time to heal ourselves to a balanced state, so that we can access and clearly process the information that exists in the connective energy that flows through all. We will then know the truth of what is for the greater good or not. We will gain confidence to stand up for ourselves, seeing ourselves as an important part of life. We will regain our freedom. Right now, our freedom is a con and our wealth is not true abundance.

It's time we all pulled together as one species. Our places of worship should be in one local building accepting the good of all religions combined under one roof. We should share and accept each other's traditions, not condemning them. We should mould our own ways to fit with each other without intimidation, but in a way that is acceptable to all.

The whole point is to balance every aspect of ourselves and our lives. Our mind, body and soul working together as one. Once we can achieve balance, we can balance the whole world. Never sit at home thinking you can't make a difference in the world, because you can. As soon as we all pull together and stand together as one, there will be peace and heaven on earth.

We build our roads, so we should say where the yellow lines go if any. The land belongs to all of us, so we should say where we want to build our homes. We came from the earth, we should be able to walk freely on it. At the moment we are paying money into machines, to park our cars and walk freely through small contained pastures of woodland. We may as well be paying to use our own feet.

Start questioning life and start using the law of attraction to attract the right answers,

If you seek the truth, you will find it.

The sad thing is that without all this negativity in our lives, we would never truly know the beauty of love. The two have to co-exist. The positive and negative have existed from the beginning of time in our building blocks forming life.

Of course there have been good intentions somewhere, but when we try to control things it really can go wrong. Every person is unique, every situation is different and of course everything is constantly changing. Yet we keep trying to control things. We find it hard enough knowing what's best for ourselves so how on earth can we think we know what is best for everyone else. Even if something felt right, give it a year and it could feel totally different. No one can take care of this world and everyone everything in it better than nature itself. All control does is restrict our natural flow in nature.

RELIGION, MYTHS AND LEGENDS

The myths and legends of old seem to be such crazy, unbelievable stories containing Dragons and Cyclopes. Things that just don't exist today and are quite unbelievable for us to comprehend. So how is it that these stories and biblical stories have lasted this long? Were they real or make believe? Well as archaeologists discover more and more, it seems to be that even though these stories have changed or exaggerated slightly over time. They have originated from fact. If we go back to prehistoric times, everything was much larger. Probably due to the more time it had to evolve before being wiped out, or possibly due to the atmosphere and gravity being slightly different than it is now. Now that we have T.V. In our lives, we can get to see all the wonderful species that have come into being here on earth. From deep in rain forests, to deep down in the depths of the ocean and the most wonderful colours of species in the Great Barrier Reef. We can see the giant fossils and bones pieced together to form such gigantic species, that we just wouldn't have believed could possibly exist. We can see the giant sized whales that exist today, that we would never have come across in our lifetime. So did such things as mystical creatures exist? In all probability the answer would be yes. The more hidden writings we find, the more we find still exists hidden under the depths of the earth. Ruins of whole cities have been found and more information contained within them. The more we find out, the more we can piece together the realty to which the writings refer to. In exodus we are told of ten plagues which fell upon Egypt.

The first was the Nile turning to blood. We now know that this could have been due, to a red poisonous Algae that killed all the fish.

The second plague was an infestation of frogs. As the water was being poisoned, the frogs would have all descended on the land.

The third plague vast swarms of gnat's tormented people and animals. All the frogspawn would now be attracting vast swarms of gnats.

The fourth, vast swarms of flies fly through the land spreading disease. As many of the frogs have left the water already contaminated, they would have died on the land attracting flies.

The fifth plague, disease on the livestock - horses, donkeys, camels, cattle, sheep and goats. But those of the Israelites were unharmed. This brings us to the story of Moses who led the Israelites to the Promised Land.

The sixth plague of festering boils on people and animals throughout the land. Probably caused by a disease carried by the flies. Possibly anthrax.

The seventh. Powerful hailstones that destroyed the standing crops and any people or cattle caught outside in the storm were killed. It is possible for a ferocious storm to cause thunderbolts of lightening and fires especially in a possible climate change.

The eighth plague. Locust in such great numbers that the ground was covered, devoured any crops left over from the storm. Still today farmers struggle with swarms of locusts.

The ninth plague. Darkness fell upon the land. In the spring dessert winds blow in from the Sahara which can blow off and on for up to about 50 days, blocking out the light from the sun for days at a time.

The tenth plague was a killing of all the first born. It's possible that the first born had the job of collecting supplies that had been stored due to the storm. As it had been contaminated by all the flies, being stored would have breaded more germs. If it were the job of the first born to collect supplies from storage, they would have breathed in the most contamination from any airborne disease.

This is just an example of how myths and legends can be explained.

When we look into this further, the Egyptians related each plague to a god. The Egyptians worshipped many gods. However when Akhenaten became pharaoh he reinstated Ra the sun god who had previously been king of the gods. He claimed to be a direct descendant, renaming the sun disc to Aten, worshipping the Aten as the one and only sun god. He built an empire apart from all the others and with his queen

Nefertiti at his side, had great influence. The Egyptians interpreted the 10 plagues as a war of the gods with Aten againstall the others. Of course if all this had happened today, our perception of it would be completely different. Given what we know, we would see it as a natural disaster. With the recourses that we have now, we would probably be able to deal with it and record it as such. I'm sure as time goes on we will find all the answers too many more myths, legends and religious stories.

The Egyptians worshipped so many gods and goddesses for all types of things, basically anything that had an influence and as we know everything has an influence on everything.

Ammut 'devourer of the dead' who helped Anubis carry out judgements.

Horus god of war, sky and falcons.

Isis goddess of magic, healing and motherhood.

Even Heket goddess of frogs (frogs depicted ancient symbol of fertility) and many more.

Things have changed over time. They've gone back and forth from worshipping many to worshipping one and back to many again. It doesn't really matter who or what we worship, just as long as we have respect for something greater than ourselves. Something to help teach us right from wrong to love and not hate. It's all a way of connecting to our higher self. That energy within us, that connects to every other energy that exists. Where we came from, our very source of god consciousness

Knowing all this, I still pray to God, I still talk to spirit, I still call to Jesus, Buddha the Gods, Goddesses and many others for help in my life.

Those energies exist because we created them. So whoever, whatever you worship or have in your life right now is good, right and just as it should be. People will come in and out of your lives over time. Some with a strong influence and a determination that their way is the right way Listen to them, listen to your heart and take from it only that which feels right and good. Leave the rest behind. We don't all have to be religious. Take what you know and what you learn to be the best that you can be allow yourself to make mistakes, for it is how we learn. We have to know what we don't want, in order to know what we do want. Forgive yourself and love yourself and others will do the same when we learn to treat ourselves with love and respect, we have no trouble treating others the same way.

You know all this airy fairy nonsense we hear about today isn't so daft. It hasn't just come about now, it has always been there. I suppose we just got hung up on the need for proof and hard evidence swaying more to scientific facts, condemning religious beliefs. It's just because we developed enough to start questioning things as part of our growth and development.

The law of attraction exists in religious teachings, just as it does in science and just as it exists today. From the beginning, we hear about God and Satan. The continuing stories teach us to balance the good and bad.

When I first started to learn all this I learnt about my guides and guardians amongst angels and archangels. I even did a meditation to meet the lords of karma. To ask permission to free myself from vows I'd made in life, that had kept me chained to people so to speak. Of course it all sounds a little far fetched, but what it actually does is help free us from the things we impose upon ourselves in our own mind. I learned to let go of my children as they grew up and left home. Allowing them to be in control of their own lives. I'm always there for them if they need me, but without the need to interfere. Of course growing up my children would make jokes, about how mum would talk to the angels and had gone loopy. No matter how much they joked I noticed they would take little bits on board, so it was all worth it. The plain fact is that it worked for me. I was releasing things and coping with stressful situations, better than I ever had before. Of course this led me to working with energy and experiencing massive changes in my body. As I grasped an understanding of all this, I was then ready to look into the scientific perspective of things. Had I looked at this first, I would never had understood a thing I read. However as I read about protons, neutrons, prisms, particles and how everything seemed to have a numeric value. I could now at least grasp a vague understanding of things that had been at one time completely beyond me.

Looking at religions today. People seem to focus on the differences, rather than the similarities. Many hide behind religions using them as a reason for riots and wars. When we are out of balance ourselves, we get an unclear message from our higher mind. When people do bad things and say that god told them to do it. They are in a state of being that has had layer upon layer of hurt, pain and suffering causing them to look for a scapegoat from facing their own insecurities, fears and other emotions. When things get to the extreme it stirs up emotions in others who aren't directly involved. Isn't it time we stopped fighting over who's belief is right and who's is wrong. It's time we realised that all are acceptable, as long as they are for the highest good of all and are of love. Those who's beliefs are of love, accept others beliefs of love without discrimination. If we follow any kind of teaching or belief without a clear conscience, without love and peace in our hearts. Then we are hiding behind them and not facing up to our true self.

Shouldn't we be teaching our children, the loving factors of all religions alongside the modern day law of attraction giving them a clearer understanding? A modern day view. Opening their minds so that they are not so easily brainwashed into anger and hatred.

We are not separate any more, we are integrated we up sticks from one country, putting down roots in another. Times have changed. So now is the time to not lose what we have learnt, but to add together the good from all to teach in a modern way.

Greek mythology explains humans, in the beginning of time as having two faces, arms and legs. Humans were overpowering the gods, so their punishment was to be split in two. Into two beings, forever searching for its other half to be complete. Many of us are blind to seeing this myth as based on truth. In an unbalanced state we do tend to search for a partner to complete us. We should always keep an open mind, as stories that pass us by are often missing pieces to life's jigsaw. Earlier on we said how anti-matter and matter collided, annihilating each other. Turning into energy, which runs through every living thing. We said how energies must be in balance and that we are all equal, no matter what our gender to the outside world may be. This myth seems to be giving us this same information, in a less complicated way.

Trying to bring the scientific into language that can be understood without all the scientific terminology. The moral stating that we are powerful beings just like 'God 'If we can search within for the balance of our masculine and feminine energies (positive / negative) and succeed in getting this right. Then we become the god of our self. This myth could also be stating that we have an opposing mate. In order for us to fit with 'the one' person that truly fits us, we must first seek balance. If we find that other half to us, we must first be a complete whole in our self. If we are not, built up fears will be immensely mirrored. Pushing and pulling each other in different directions. In comes the law of attraction again. Only when we have attracted everything that can teach us life's lessons. To help rid us of fear so that we are able to face every issue that has come up against us. Only then can we attract our full self-back to us in another. We are all striving for love, peace and happiness. We must first strive to be balanced, only then will true abundance follow.

We have given god the name 'God' and also the opposite 'Devil'. We have created the idea. We follow a certain set religion, trying to be the best that we can be. We live our lives by rules and regulations, fearing our judgement day. We push our own fears onto others stating that they should live their lives a certain way. That is because the other person is living in fear and so they create it. We have programmed ourselves to believing that God is a male gender. So then as evolution has progressed. Man is more powerful than woman. In times gone by women were seen and not heard, staying at home looking after the house and children. Their voice never to be heard and never as strong as the male. Is this because the male was physically stronger? Is this why we see god as male form? If God was man then who created him?

God is not a person, god is a balanced energy of both man and woman. Positive and negative God is the protector and nurturer. The strong and loving that is what we all can be if we look within, face our self and realise the power that we all hold.

In the beginning of god's creation, man and woman were made. Eve was created from Adams rib. The two were to live in bliss in the Garden of Eden for the rest of their time. On the one condition of not eating the forbidden fruit Of course Satan (devil) convinced eve to take the fruit. Eve was then punished by God. Both Adam and Eve were no longer to live in bliss and harmony.

Remember that good voice and bad voice within us. The positive and negative to everything in life. The law of attraction that runs through us all. If we do something that is bad or harmful to ourselves or another, it will surely come back round to us. Every action has a reaction. Holy teachings have been around way before we could scientifically prove things. Yet holy teachings are the law of attraction. This could be why some of the stories are hard to believe or even hard to understand, which is why they get given the name 'myth'. Science then proves the findings, but then how can we understand? When science itself is another language to us, using names and words that we are not familiar with. Science is describing and finding out more about us all the time. It's just that many cannot relate this into our everyday lives. Eve could not resist the temptation and was too curious to live in a balanced state. We read this as though Eve has then put the whole of humanity at risk, all of us being punished for the rest of time. We live in fear thinking that we cannot change certain situations. Believing in bad energy by name of the Devil. This is not so. Eve made a mistake because she wanted to push the boundaries. It's human nature. All it teaches is that whichever voice we listen to, whether it be good or bad. It will come back to us because it is what we have created. Again the law of attraction states that, we attract to us that which we are. That which we feel and think about this part of the holy teaching is also showing that we all started off in a balanced state. It is going through life, living in fear and negative behaviour that keeps us from reaching this state of being once again. We more often than not seem to hit rock bottom before turning things around for ourselves. Only when we know all that we don't want, do we strive to get back to that which we do want in our lives. Furthermore, Eve being made from Adams rib. Shows that in every woman, there is a masculine energy and in every man there is a feminine energy. It's ok to make mistakes, but to better our lives we must be able to see where we go wrong. We must be able to see the lesson coming back round for us to break free from old habits, enabling us to live free and happy balanced lives.

This is just a story to help us understand the law of attraction and that we are all equal. Back when the story was written there may not have been the technology to explain this in a way that could be understood. So it was with good old imagination that brought the story to life.

God stands for good and devil stands for evil. One has +1 letter and the other has -1 letter. Therefore one is positive and the other is negative. We haven't just created them, they have created us.

We put rules and regulations in place to help keep ourselves in line, because some of us push the boundaries too far. This tips us way out of balance. We then start to hear the negative voice over the positive. Convincing ourselves that god has told us to do bad things, when in actual fact it is our own mind telling us what to do. There is a fine line between love and hate between right and wrong, crazy and genius. All we can do is our best, living life the way we choose. Many of us are existing in life and not living. We fail to see the abundance that surrounds us. Some think they have all the time in the world while others wish it away. Some get high on adrenaline rushes all the way through life, while others work to live and often live in fear.

When the power of love becomes balanced for all, we will overcome our love of power. Many of us have grown up believing that authority is the truth. It is time for our truth to become our authority.

What makes a specific group of people capable of laying down and imposing rules upon others? Why on earth would any good person want to control another? We have a hard enough task keeping ourselves on the straight and narrow. So why on earth would we think that we are capable of controlling someone we don't know as well as we know ourselves?

How did we ourselves get to such a state, where others are controlling our every move?

It seems that those wonderful stories created by religions are a great way of keeping control. By getting us to believe things, we will as good as impose rules upon ourselves. We condemn others who question our beliefs, believing that we are following the right way and others are wrong. Of course we believe our way is the right way, because that is what we have been led to believe. The crazy thing is that when we look more closely at religions, their stories have derived from ancient teachings that were possibly telling the story of nothing more than astrology. Going back to Horus the god of light. This was the name given to the sun that rises each day giving light and life as everything grows the sun travels across the sky as it rises up each morning and sets in the evening. As winter drawers in it appears less and less, until it stops still before moving up slightly in the sky. This is the story of the son of god who performed miracles, who died and was resurrected. The same story can be told for Attis of Greece, Krishna in India Mithra in Persia and many more. Even the birth sequence follows the star in the cast known as Sirius which lines up with three stars known as orions belt or in the birth of Jesus the three kings. When this happens they point to where the sun rises therefore the birth of the sun or son of god. The mother Mary represents the constellation Virgo Later on Jesus has twelve apostles representing the twelve constellations as they follow the sun.

So what good is it doing for us to focus our beliefs on such stories? We're taught that god loves us and protects us if we follow his commandments. He resembles that all powerful, all knowing, perfect wisdom which is our higher mind. Of course there's a problem, we now see our higher mind as a god in the sky and we've stopped listening to that godly source from within us. We now listen to what other people teach us, thinking they are spreading god's word. We are leaving ourselves wide open to manipulation. Those in power can hide behind religions to get away with answering difficult questions. Ask too many questions and before we know it we are blaspheming. Now people can really start to manipulate the situation. Pass yourself off as one religion, attacking another and before we know it riots and wars are breaking out. Use the media right and people in power can create threats of terror controlling the whole world. Before we know it we are getting involved in fighting wars that we originally disagreed with. Believe it or not it all comes down to money, greed, power and control. Is it possible that all this corruption is really going on in the world? Where is all our money going? We pay a tremendous amount of tax yet it's never enough. We're constantly raising funds for charities, yet it doesn't seem to make much of a difference. We're given just enough information to make us think we know what's going on in the world, without causing us to ask too many questions. Do we really know all there is to know, or are we being kept in the dark? Let's face it, we're all too busy to have time to think about it all. We just go along with paying bills and taxes even if we don't agree with it, after all there are so many rules. We don't stand a chance of fighting back, because authority has spoken. Who is authority? Authority isn't our protector. Authority throws us in prison if we don't follow the rules, no matter what we know to be just and fair. We receive bills off most people yet we receive demands off our councils and governments. Failure to pay their money, causes them to demand the whole lot when they know you can't manage an instalment. So they'll just take you straight to court, because somehow they can afford to do that. How long will we sit around and let people trample on us like this. When will we realise that we are important enough to put ourselves first?

Time is an illusion, it is another scientific measurement from when the sun rises until the sun sets. Just like our age, that is measured by time. Many of us think we have time. We go through life wishing the days away, the weekend cannot come fast enough. Each year goes quicker, the older we get and the same things have happened almost repeatedly. We lose sight of our interests and passions focusing on all that is wrong in our lives. The routine of negative behavior becomes our comfort zone we get bored or frustrated, leading us to more negative behaviour and so it goes on. So what if we told you that it's time to live. There's no time like the present dream big and follow your heart. Gain your wisdom through life's lessons and never stop believing in yourself. You are a powerful being you deserve all the abundance in the world. Time will not wait for you, push out of your comfort zone. Get to know yourself, face your fears. Know your passions, explore your strengths and weaknesses. Open your eyes to what a beautiful place the world actually is. Open your mind to understanding everyone's views and show compassion in all that you do. The biggest regrets, are always that which we haven't done in life. So play around with life, take the highs with the lows and experience all which you have wanted to. If you fall, pick yourself up and dust yourself off. You are in control, create what you want in life always considerate of others. You create your life, so you can handle it. If you couldn't make the challenges in life, you wouldn't set yourself up for them. We have to realise that we possess the ability, to get through any situation in life. As long as everything we do has a balance of love for our self, others and the universe as a whole. Anything is possible. Never, ever allow yourself to take on others negative behaviours. We all have our problems, we all go through bad times. We can all come through them with positive outlooks and reasons to why that part of our journey went the way it did. So tell your story and start today, with a knowing that you will receive everything that you want in life. Don't get to the end of your time with regrets. Keep your faith, love yourself and believe in yourself. Life is a fantastic game, so let's start playing it right.

EVOLUTION

We're pretty amazing creatures if you think about It But how on earth did we come to be the amazing beings that we are today? Through evolution the very thing that drives us forward, moulding, adapting and shaping the things to come. There are many stories and theories. Unless we can see hard evidence for ourselves, who knows what to believe. What we do know is that we do change over time. Of course in a lifetime we won't see much evidence of this at all, in comparison to the bigger picture. Look around at the creatures surrounding us. Some have developed wings to fly. Others have not even developed eyes to see with and yet their bodies have developed to their own surroundings, in a way that they can manage without them. Many have stayed in the sea while others have adapted to stay on land, with lungs that can breath air and legs with feet to get around on. Some sleep through the winter while others migrate to warmer climates. Many create their own weapons, while we create ours from other components of the earth. There are creatures that can adapt their colour, look and texture to their surroundings. They make themselves invisible to predators. Many even have their own fluorescent lights. Some produce poisonous venom that kills and others paralyse. We on the other hand seem to make ours by learning from these amazing creatures.

Whatever we need, we use and develop. Those who have lost the use of a part of their bodily functions, will use that energy that is no longer needed to develop other parts of their body to compensate. There are also those of us, who on focusing too much energy on our brains for instance. Will not have enough energy to stay fit and healthy, especially if we are not putting into our bodies the right food for fuel. Poor food choices mean that our digestive system, uses more fuel to digest food before we've even started. That which we don't use eventually disappears. We may start to notice aches and pains as we slowly deteriorate. It makes sense to think that we were more than likely to be more like other animals. As far as being more alert, with our main senses a lot keener than they are today.

Even now I see how different my children are, to when we were growing up. Our parents knew what all the plants were round and about, they knew what could be used and what would give you a poorly stomach.

Today we rely more and more on others for things, as we focus more on one particular thing ourselves. It seems that for us to achieve anything now, we have to put all our time and effort into one area. In order to be as good, if not better than everyone else before us. Supermarkets mean we don't have to use our sense of smell to pick food from the earth, as we rely on someone else's knowledge to do that for us. We don't use our instincts in the same way that animals do, because we don't have a constant threat from major predators. With that our hearing and eyesight seem to weaken, as we get older and less curious. Because we don't have to be so alert constantly, we are more relaxed as far as listening and we don't have to constantly look for food and predators. Because we don't have to search for food in the old way, we now sit at computers evolving our brains in new ways while our bodies move around less. Cars, lifts escalators, conveyor belts even computer games. Our brains work harder using up our energy, while our bodies suffer the consequences. Even computers and machinery, are taking over the jobs of the more physical amongst us. On realizing the downfalls to our new ways of life, we are now encouraged to go to gyms, classes and take up some type of sport for fun or entertainment The trouble with these is that they become mundane Living a physical life gives us constant change however small, keeping it more interesting.

We seem to have tipped completely out of balance our ego that drives us forward has lost sight of reality, as far as our need to survive. We are now greedy for lavish things that we do not necessarily need. Using money to exchange things hasn't helped. If we go back in time, the poor amongst us exchanged goods and shared more we recycled by way of making things to last and passing or selling them on to others. Everyone seemed to lend and borrow each other's belonging this wasn't a problem as much as today, because people new the value of things and took care of them. Of course today, more and more we develop a stigma towards using and buying second hand goods. Things are made so cheaply, quickly and easily today that they don't have the same value. If something breaks, it is quicker and easier to throw an Item away and buy a new one. We don't realise that we are slowly developing in a way that is having a horrendous effect on the earth. The very thing that sustains our life is being wrecked, at an extremely fast pace. This is all because, each and every single person on the planet has a minute effect. However when so many of us behave in the same way. That minute effect becomes massive. The more we want the more others provide. Trouble is when we rely on others to supply a massive demand, we fail to see when things are going wrong. We presume that we are still eating healthy food when we purchase it, from larger cheaper stores. Putting the smaller everyday business man out of work, as he cannot compete with the low prices. We close our eyes and ears to how these larger supermarkets, can supply so much so cheap. We not only restrict ourselves from the freedom of our earth, we contain every other living thing that we possibly can. Great masses of animals are kept together in small proximities, without freedom to even move about let alone roam free. Some of these used to feed on grass, now they're lucky if they get to stand on or even see any. So if these animals aren't eating healthy as they naturally should. What on earth are we eating when we buy them off the shelves in supermarkets? Of course there's more than just food at stake here. Were so desperate to learn and push others to keep up, that we want paper by the bulk we constantly want change in our lives and want new furniture amongst other things. Because of this, rain forests are slowly disappearing. Causing a devastating effect on the ozone layer and that's just for starters. We have to balance ourselves and the way we evolve before it's too late.

We've evolved this far from just a tiny cell. Are we really prepared to mess it up now? It's amazing to see what we have evolved from and the length of time it has taken us. We can look at fossils of the first creatures that evolved into being the very building blocks of ourselves. Before we'd even developed bones, arms and legs. It's amazing to think that such fossils from the Cambrian era have survived over such a vast time. Fossils that hadn't even developed a digestive system which contains a stomach. Let alone a brain. So think about it, if we had actually started to evolve and hadn't yet developed a brain. What actually developed us in the first place...? Our higher mind perhaps. That almighty God that connects and creates us all. That one being from which we all came from?

We're still evolving, so let's try and get it right. We are always going to want change in our lives, even though most of us think we don't as we hold ourselves back from things with fear. It's the thing that keeps us evolving and adapting. We look around at all these computers and advancing technology, wondering how we'll ever keep up and yet we do. First it was money, then banks and cheques. Now it's computer transactions, yet we all have to move forward with the process at some sort of pace. Even If we're sat in our homes content, after a while we will feel the need to get rid of an old item and replace it with something new or different. Or we may just add something extra, from a small ornament to a new item of clothing or even a lick of paint on the walls. We have to have an interest in something even if it's food or a thirst for knowledge. It's what keeps us moving forward. If we were to have absolutely nothing we would grow stagnant and just lose the will to live. We just need to learn to balance our need to evolve. We're Just one person in a whole world full, so we think that what we do as a single being doesn't really affect the rest of the world. Ever told a secret. Or even heard one about someone you don't even know that well it happens and it just goes to show, the ripple effect that things can have. People copy, its part of our learning process. Before you know it anything you do first, someone else is doing after you and so on. The point to all this is that if we keep wanting and getting like we do, our focus is on the wrong things for the wrong reasons i.e. Don't need it. Just want it, let it sit there for a length of time then throw it. Not share it, not lend it or not give it. Then others out there are going to supply it and if it makes money then it doesn't matter what negative effects are caused to create it. If we stay ignorant then we feel we are not to blame. After all it's the ones at the top of the chain that cause all the main problems. They do it because we let them and not only that but because we want them to. Because we don't care where things come from, or what negative effects were caused to produce and supply things. Why should they be any different Things will only change fast enough if we all change our ways. We are not responsible for other people, but we are responsible for ourselves. We do affect the balance of life and evolution however small, of course we can't suddenly change our habits. That would be like telling a shy person to suddenly be confident, but we can start reprogramming our brains with positive books and programs. We can start healing ourselves to release all the blocked energy that tips us out of balance causing pain and illness. We can strive to balance ourselves, so in time we bring more balance to the planet earth.

Throughout all our evolution, we seem to have imposed more and more rules upon ourselves. We're losing sight of what's necessary and important to us as individuals. From an early age we are unnaturally torn away from our parents and pushed into an environment with strangers. New rules already being imposed upon us. Before we know it, we are being pushed to learn things that we are not necessarily interested in. Learning things at pace that isn't natural for the individual. We are all interested in learning different things at different times, yet we are forced to sit through lesson after lesson even if we are not interested. We are forced into close constant proximity with others on a daily basis. Some of these we are comfortable with and others who make our lives miserable from day to day, yet we have no free will to remove ourselves from the situation or their proximity. We lose the comfort and security of our parents before we are ready. Leaving us to learn and cope with new and ongoing relationships. Relationships, something we struggle with as adults. Yet we expect our children to learn and cope without us by their side for protection, or to run back to when in need of a little security. From an early age we are pushing ourselves too far, too fast. Is it any wonder our children are so stressed at such a young age? Any wonder we make so many mistakes building stress and habits layer upon layer. By the time we're at an age of breaking free from our parents to make our own way in the world, we've built up so many barriers we don't really understand ourselves any more. The transition from leaving our parents side, was such an unnatural process. That by the time we go from being a child to an adult, is it any wonder we tend to go off the rails. Our emotions are so far buried that when they finally find a release, they tip the scales way off balance. From there as we go on to learn about life in the big wide world, unsure of what we're doing and how we feel. We then wonder why we are so easily brainwashed into doing wrong. We've never been allowed to do right by ourselves, so how on earth can we know how to do right by others.

<u>SCIENCE</u>

Science is like another language to many of us. We are finding out that there is more to life than, that which we can see with the naked eye. Therefore new words are made for constant new findings. We then find these new findings have totally different behaviour patterns, to that which we already know. So more complicated words and phrases are created to help explain.

The Big Bang theory

In the beginning god created the heavens and the earth and so it began with the Big Bang

We still don't know fully how it all started. At the moment, we have to kind of by into the concept that something was created from nothing. Of course, what is nothing?

Here is what we think we know in its simplest form:

Everything that exists was at a point so dense, that it expanded. First came the expansion of space, created by quantum fluctuations. Then came the light from the chemical elements we call electrons. As the universe expanded it cooled causing these elements to clump together creating quarks. Quarks created protons and neutrons and the list goes on, until we end up with all that exists today.

The point is that all these particles are the building blocks of matter and matter formed everything we know that takes up space. So of course these building blocks carried on evolving and shaping the whole solar system, bashing into each other and clumping together. Before we know it, we have large planets spinning like vortices gravitationally pulling things in and holding things in place. When all the ingredients are right the planet carries on developing until we have life as we know it today. Of course that matter has now expanded including air, water, plants, animals and all that we can see including us. What we are realising is that matter does not exist without mind to define it. Mind is the energy that runs through everything, this brings us back to god. This energy was created from one point and expanded with both positive and negative (good and bad, god and satan). It flows through all that exists. It holds us in place (the law of gravity). Don't forget our brains are only a part of the process, as these were not in existence from the beginning. They are something we have developed later on. If our brains didn't cause us to evolve, then something else did.

Understanding that everything including the air that we breathe is matter and made up of microscopic particles that cannot be seen by the naked eye. Knowing that some form of energy runs through all matter, can help us understand how everything is connected as one. Don't forget we came from one point and expanded. We haven't necessarily separated, because we are still connected by something. Just because we can't see it does not mean that it doesn't exist.

Everything we see and everything we can't see, contains the same building blocks i.e. the same microscopic particles from the beginning of time as we know it.

Scientists use the things we have and know of today. They develop and create machinery such as microscopes and telescopes. They work backwards breaking everything down until they get to the smallest particles. As they find out how these things work, they can go on to create even more, allowing us to find out how everything works together. Before all this happens, something has to set the process in motion. That thing is just a simple thought. That thought develops into a theory and as we know many scientists have been mocked for their theories. That is until they can prove their theories are right. Christopher Columbus went against everyone thinking the world was flat, proving that the world was round and gravity holds us in place. From here we have developed, to being able to film and photograph. Not just our own planet, but also others in the solar system. We now have microscopes that can see not only the particles that we knew existed, but also the particles that create those particles and so on. At this moment in time, we are unable to see into a black hole. Yet the theory has been set in place, that if we can create a telescope as big as the world. It may be possible to see into a black hole.

On relaxing in the sun, it is possible to see what look to be tiny particles of light. On trying to focus on one particle I have found that it is impossible to do. They are always slightly out of central vision. On moving my eyes left, the particles will do the same or disappear. On looking up, they will move up or disappear and so on.

Particles have now been found that cannot be contained. Scientists are now having to use magnetic fields to hold them in position for examination.

Again we are brought back to magnetism and gravity that exists in the law of attraction.

Everything has an opposing force, electrons are identical to positrons, yet electrons have a negative force while positrons have a positive force. We have matter and antimatter which is made up of atoms and anti-atoms. They are all mirror images of each other, just as we are mirror images of each other. Electricity has a positive charge and a negative charge. Everything seems to have an identical partner with an opposing force, causing that push and pull creating the law of attraction. As our thought waves are matter, they too are made up of these gravitational pushing pulling forces. The law of gravity is what holds our universe and everything in it, in place. It is the force that affects nature, from the oceans tide to our emotions and circulatory system. Even within ourselves we are made up of positive and negative elements, which are masculine and feminine. These are the things we need to balance to become at peace with ourselves and each other. We are like mini universes ourselves containing vortices (chakras) that draw in energy and information for our brains to process, in order to keep the rest of our mini solar system (our bodies) in working order.

On balancing the positive and negative energy within us and within all the particles that make up our whole being. We are able to slow down and flow in life's synchronicity. Doing this enables us to reconnect fully with the rest of our existence, therefore the rest of our universe. The whole universe holds the answers to all our questions. What happens is this. Someone picks up a thought from the universe and all that has happened from the beginning of time. They contemplate on this thought, asking questions until they develop a theory. From here they decide they want to know more, using the law of attraction they attract all the answers and proof they need. As we can only process the information that we are ready for. The flow of life will take us in different directions learning and growing until we are capable of processing the information that we seek. You wouldn't give a child complicated arithmetic until they've learnt the basics. Just the same, the law of attraction teaches us the basics first. What we give out comes back to us. As it comes back to us we can decide, if it is something we want or something we don't want. When we give out, we are actually giving to another part of ourselves. This is why the lesson comes back to us. By showing someone else love, we are actually showing ourselves love. Everyone out there acts like a mirror, reflecting everything we give out back to us.

Telepathy and mediumship, doesn't seem so crazy anymore. All clairvoyants do is develop this connection going back to the way we were as babies, before learning to speak words. The more we use speech as a way of communicating the more we stop using our natural way of communicating using our hidden senses. We start rushing around forgetting to listen to those thoughts in our head. We stop noticing our feelings of emotions as we pick up those feelings of others. Before we know it we've lost the ability to understand our own emotions, let alone the emotions of others. We all have the ability to reconnect. We can see now that the law of attraction exists not only around us, but through us and through everything that has been created. It is now proving to be more than just a thought. It is matter and it does exist. It's time we all stopped complaining and start listening to the universe. It speaks to us, all we have to do is learn to quieten our minds and listen. There is no greater teacher, than that greater part of us.

We all seem to want to know where we have come from and why we are the way we are, why people act the way they do. Why people say the things they say and how science can give us the answers. If only we could all understand science simply and uncomplicated. Most of us know that the planets orbit the sun. This is because the sun has the greatest mass, it is the largest, heaviest object in our solar system. Because of this it has the strongest gravitational pull. On first perceptions we would expect the planets to be suctioned into the sun and yet they stay in their positions surrounding it. The reason for this is simply because of the way they themselves are travelling. They each have their own orbit which is their path held by gravity. Any planets with orbits that crossed, have already collided until we are left with those we have today. To give you an idea of how this works, if you tie a weight on the end of a length of string and rotate the string. The weight will orbit without falling to your hand.

The sun is a star. We need the sun as part of our survival as we ourselves are made from stars. Let's go back to the Big Bang for a moment to the protons and neutrons. These particles clumped together under gravity to form helium nuclei and hydrogen nuclei now were starting to get to words we are familiar with. The gasses created by these elements clumped together to form stars. The gas clumps together and becomes so hot that light is emitted. When a star runs out of elements to create energy It collapses in on itself, as it can no longer support its gravity. When this happens matter is spewed out as the star dies.

There is only so much matter that has created our solar system. Death is a part of life. If we all lived forever constantly reproducing the world would become over crowded. The matter which created the earth would eventually be destroyed by the human race. Eventually the earth would most probably blow up and the whole of our species would be wiped out. This is why we believe in reincarnation. If bodies are matter and they go back into the ground, the cells are still present. If our soul is energy, then it cannot die. In the law of physics, energy cannot be made nor unmade. Therefore it already exists and lives on. If energy is held in the body through magnetic forces, then this is why the law of attraction will run through us. Also why our thought patterns are so important, because the mind controls matter.

We are an intelligence that keeps evolving through the ages. Every subject in life is there to help us put the pieces together, to get the answers to the bigger picture.

Life is an illusion created by the mind. Mind controls subatomic particles. These are tiny specks of matter that interact with each other. They created us and they create what our minds choose to create. We have the power to create good in our lives and also the power to create bad. Energy flows through our bodies. In a good state it flows freely, keeping our bodies in perfect working order. As we take on stress the energy becomes blocked building pressure on our matter (body), causing pain and malfunctions resulting in illness. As our higher mind already has the ability to fix and repair our bodies (i.e. when we cut our skin it automatically heals) our mind can accelerate the process and repair further damage when illness seems to have got out of control. When we take on stress and become trapped in our own cycle of fear, we tend to focus on any pain and suffering which we may feel. Giving our attention to this creates more, so an illness can spread or get worse. When we finally decide that it isn't going to beat us and we decide to fight it. We start to hold it at bay or diminish it. Everything is an illusion that we create and control. It is tiny subatomic particles held in place by gravity (more subatomic particles) which are controlled by the mind.

The mind can be used to remove the blocked negative energy that we created. However when it has been removed, it leaves a void. This void causes pain also, as matter needs energy to flow through it. To remove the pain we need to fill it with energy, vibrating with a positive charge Therefore love. As everything is a vibration of subatomic particles, we can use speech and symbols to add to the vibrational charge.

Of course we don't just create illness with the negative energy that we create. The more negative energy we create, the more that energy seems to control us. As the chakras in the body become blocked they are unable to process the positive information in the body. When negatively charged emotions are suppressed in the body, the body starts to malfunction and the scales start to tip. Different parts of the suppressed energy starts to find a release. This can be with bouts of aggression or floods of tears. There can be a mass serge of energy, which then leaves the body deflated. Different personalities arise and show themselves at different times, in its most drastic form schizophrenia. Luckily most of us only get as far as showing another side to our character when we drink alcohol even at the point of no return, I do believe we all possess the ability to repair and cure ourselves. The question is do we want to? Earlier on we said that we are the matter created from stars, as when they die they spew out all the elements of matter which clump together to form the planets.

If we find it hard to understand the stars themselves, we've only to look within or around at the generations of beings that have been. A young star will spin around fast, where as an old star will slow down with age. Just like the human race, some of the very first stars were created as twins. Yes, a gas cloud actually made two stars from one formation. Some of us create twins from the same egg that we hold within the womb. By understanding ourselves and the human body, it can help us understand the creation of the universe and of new things that we create.

Could this be the reason why so many of us look to the sky for comfort, or on losing a loved one? Wondering if the person or people we lose are the bright stars in the sky. You see science proves the ideas that we have. Even when we don't understand science, we can listen to our intuition to find the answers to our being here. Even in science every element, particle and atom has an opposite, mirror or twin. Before the advancement of science and technology, intuition and imagination were the only tools we had. Hence all the myths and stories we here of today. Our time was spent analysing nature, watching the sun rise and set. Figuring out the positions. Watching the world go from day to night, light to dark. Gazing at the stars, how they are positioned mapping out the night sky. Nature has given us everything we need to know and live off. We create earth's time from the sun. We can also see matter and antimatter creating energy. When we watch positively charged clouds come into contact with negatively charged clouds, creating thunder and lightning.

Astrology was studied in ancient times, split into twelve segments for each month of the year every star group in the sky depicted an animal shape. The word zodiac is a Greek word meaning the circle of animals. For every zodiac sign there developed a myth as to how and why they had a place in the stars. Birth charts are discovered when the earth moves in and out of the twelve segments, giving us a ruling sign. We are born with a bigger magnetic push and pull from the stars and planets that are closest to earth. This has an influence on the elements that form and create us at birth. We will all remember, all the stories about the world coming to an end in 2012. This was just a shift from one age to another. As we saw the end of the Piscean age, we moved into the beginning of the Aquarian age. This shift had been predicted in ancient times. As language hadn't been developed and early writings were in hieroglyphics. The pictures and symbols could be misinterpreted. We saw much evidence of this as fear and panic seemed to be all anyone talked about, leading up to the event.

Astrology is a great help in understanding ourselves. Many agree and many do not, as we don't tend to all look into the details of our creation. We look at the night sky thinking that everything is to far away to have an effect. We don't tend to realise the sheer size of what we can actually see. Our observations are of tiny glimmering specks in the night sky and our perceptions can be very deceptive. Many of us look to astrology to determine our future. We check the latest magazines to see what is in the stars. We rely on others to predict our future, often thinking we cannot change the outcome. Remember the law of attraction. If we think and feel that someone else's point of view is correct about our own lives, then that is what we will attract. A medium will pick up what you are creating with your thoughts and actions right now. It's always possible to change some things. We do not have to allow what exists in the now to determine our future. We do not have to read newspapers and listen to the news believing that they determine the way life is taking us. We have the power to change things or make a difference. If we sit waiting for our future to come to us we are wishing our lives away, hoping for a fantastic ending and doing nothing to get to there. We all have our own very unique mind. It's time we started using it without following other people's views and answers as to who we are. Maybe so many of us do this because we are afraid of failing but we are also afraid of succeeding.

Once again it comes down to getting the balance right. Getting back to the law of attraction. Every cell and muscle contained in our body has a memory. After so long doing the same thing, for example; smoking which is a negative behaviour pattern or exercise which is positive behaviour. It becomes encoded into our muscles and cells. Even when we are used to getting up in the morning at the same time. After years of doing this our bodies become used to the action. Take it away, the body and mind will react. Chemicals such as endorphins are released in the brain making us feel happy and stimulated. Take something away abruptly and we feel we are missing something our frustrations build up and we blame our behaviour on the way we feel, as we have imbalanced our production of happy chemicals. This is how we get addicted to such things like caffeine, exercise or work etc. because as soon as we stop we don't have a clue what to do with ourselves. Our muscles remember the feelings of the reoccurring movement and our mind has now lost its focus. What we fail to realise, is that even when we exercise regularly or even obsessively. Although this is a positive behaviour, we are still using this to the extremity to take our minds from our own fears and emotions. We follow routine rather than the flow of life. If we never face ourselves, how can we ever use the law of attraction in a positive manner and attract our hearts desire. How can we ever reach a point of true abundance and happiness?

To this day the universe is still expanding. It is not known when it will stop or what will happen once it reaches the end, if there is an end. Just like the Big Bang. Our evolution started off slow and has progressed faster and faster. We are now evolving at a much greater speed. It seems to be the same with everything in life. Writing this book started slowly and as time went by it seemed to progress faster right up until the end. Then what happens is this, the end seems to take forever. Time seems to stand still. As children, adults often told us to enjoy our youth, as time would fly the older we got. Today the younger generations are picking up technology so quickly. They seem to overtake the older generations. Using the older generation's knowledge to speed up their own new advances. Now here's a thought. What would happen if we reach our full evolutional state of being? If the whole of humanity became completely balanced and fully evolved? Would we have an effect on the rest of universe? Would we stop expanding in the way we are at the moment? Would we have all our answers including those, as to what dark matter and dark energy are?

Maybe the universe will expand to infinity, or maybe it will stop expanding as we stop evolving. Is it possible that once we are fully balanced, the energy of the earth is fully balanced? If that were so, would it then be possible that the energy of the whole universe would be balanced? If this were to happen would we then be in a state where the magnetism from our universe, would attract other universes of the same balance. Does the law of attraction exist throughout infinity? What if we are pushing away other universes because we are out of balance? If the whole universe was a balanced energy, would it attract another universe of the same frequency just like people?

<u>LOVE</u>

Picture two groups of children in a school playground. One child goes from one group to the other spreading rumours. We've all come across it, when someone tells us that someone has said something nasty about us only to later find out that it either hadn't been said at all, or has been put across in a totally different context. The backbiting starts and the person spreading the rumours either stands back enjoying the drama they have caused, or stays involved enjoying being a part of it. Of course this is in its mildest form. Now let's look at it in its worst form.

When jobs are scarce, we are enticed in to service by way of being paid to learn new skills. We enter army's, police forces and others similar, expecting new opportunities. Believing that if we are called into action, it will be to protect our own from wrong doers. When the time comes to fight we do not realise that we are at war with innocent manipulated people. We fail to see that the people that we work for, who stay hidden behind the scenes. Are possibly planning and consorting with the enemy, to create the bloodshed.

This all goes to show that no matter how innocent we start out. As we take on stress during our lives, we all struggle with the imbalance caused. If we are not brought up in the right nurturing environment, even the most innocent can turn to the extreme negative behaviour. This is why we have no right to judge even the most corrupt behaviours, as we all are guilty of some imperfection however slight. Two wrongs don't make a right and negative behaviour will never cancel out negative behaviour. The two energies (positive and negative) have to be balanced. We can only be responsible for our own behaviour, therefore balancing our own energies. When we can heal ourselves to the stage of balancing our own emotions, we can have an effect on the people around us through the law of attraction. It took an extremely long time to get to this stage in evolution. For us all to wake up, heal and become balanced it will take an extremely long time also, but as we have already learned. Time goes faster until the end. When we get to the end in a balanced state, it will seem to last forever.

To hold hate within us towards another, will only create hate in our own lives. To forgive an enemy, we must be able to understand them. To make a difference to the world, we need to make a difference in ourselves by focusing on love. When we learn to balance the love for ourselves with our love for others, it enables us to use our own mind to its full potential. When our focus is on that which is best for us, such as our bodies being fit and healthy. We will refrain from fueling our bodies with substances that disease and illness thrive off. If everyone in the world looked after and accepted every part of themselves. Illness such as cancer would be reduced. We would not need to constantly fund charities as we think we are doing. Therefore reducing the amount of money circulating into the wrong hands, funding the wrong things. As we remove the funds for warfare and army's. Those behind it all, will eventually have to start fighting their own battles. When it is finally possible for this to come about. We will not be coming back from war scarred for life with mental health issues. We cannot control money, if we are not the ones making it. However we can start to control our use of it. If we buy into the concept of money, we fuel all that is done with it. We need to learn to stand up for ourselves and say 'no' when it matters.

We need to realise that we are in control of ourselves. Most importantly we need to wake up and realise the power and potential that we all hold within. Say 'no' to wars, violence, hatred and fear. Say 'yes' to peace, happiness, love and abundance.

REALISING OUR DREAMS

We all have dreams, no matter how big or small. When we dream we are taken in different directions to grow and learn, so we are able to achieve those dreams. Because we hit hardship as part of life's lessons, we often fail to see that they are part of the journey towards our dream. Believing we are failing, we stop striving for the dream. We can find ourselves listening to the naysayers, who are only speaking from their own fears. These people may also have failed to see the reality of the journey towards their own dreams. If something fails or falls through. It is always because something better is around the corner. We sometimes mistake the stepping stones for the real dream, believing it has failed. Of course balance seems to be the key to everything, but on looking a little deeper there is another key which seems to help the scales of life stabilise and that is love. Open your heart and you truly will find all the answers. So it seems that if we all open our hearts and look a little deeper, beyond all the hurt, pain, habits and pent up emotions. We're actually deep down all very lovely people. Yes all of us and yes that most definitely includes you! So give yourself a part on the back for making it this far. Take a look in the mirror and tell yourself how wonderful you really are. See the real you beneath all the walls of protection that you built up over the years, the real, lovely wonderful you. Tell yourself that you are going to do right by yourself. That you will love yourself unconditionally and take care of yourself for the rest of your time here on earth. Know that you are as important as everyone else on this planet. Forgive yourself when you get it wrong. It's not wrong to be a little selfish from time to time, as long as it is with love in your heart you can't go wrong. When we take good care of ourselves, we put ourselves in a good state which can then be of help to others. Make it your mission in life to get your wonderful self back to a state of health. Free from pain and suffering free from negative mind sets which keep you from feeling wonderfully happy. Make it your mission to attract all that you need to help set you free. Freedom truly is a great abundance. You deserve to be truly happy and fulfill your dreams no matter how big or small. You are perfect just the way you are.

Your help will arrive in many forms, so keep looking and be ready for all that comes. The more you open your arms to love and accept with gratitude, the more will be bestowed upon you. Enjoy it you truly do deserve it.

Balance is the key to life.
THE END
Or is it the beginning?

ACKNOWLEDGEMENT

My deepest gratitude goes out to YOU. As you are a part of the whole universe that added to the information out there to be picked up. To every philosopher that ever had a thought. To every scientist that went out to prove their theory's. To every archeologist who helped find and uncover the hidden clues to our past. To every religious person who kept the faith. To every writer and artist for sharing. To every living soul that thought, talked, wrote, drew or sang and in doing so, added to the universal source of information. Only with your help could this book come into existence. Thank you.

AUTHOR BIOGRAPHY

Ok, so you will want to know who I am and why I, of all people, have the ability to write such a book. The most important thing is that I've suffered a little in life.

Nothing major, but enough to be able to understand what others can go through.

This is because anything we go through in life is big to ourselves, even if it seems small in comparison to someone else's problems. Allergic rhinitis since I was a child, rheumatism, depression, suicidal thoughts, stubbornness, to name but a few. I've taken tablets for most of my life, and now I have naturally healed myself to a state where I take none. For many years now, I have studied hard and learnt a lot, both physically and mentally. I have been doing workshops and courses in all different areas, giving myself a greater understanding. I personally have changed so much that I am now able to write and share what I have learnt.

As a parent I am able to see different points of views from different perspectives, both as a child and as a parent. On my journey to becoming a reiki master, I have learnt to feel old emotions examining thoughts and feelings that I have taken on as far back as the trauma of birth.

I understand the body thoroughly from an emotional point and am also able to feel sensations and pains that travel through the body triggering other parts of the body to suffer.

I can connect emotions and stress to pain, finding the root cause of illness and pain in the body. I have also experienced love of others on a completely different level. I have the ability to love absolutely anything and everything. That love has led me to writing this book, in order to help as many and as much as I possibly can.

I want to share all that I have learnt with everyone else in the world. I only got where I am today because others shared their knowledge with me. I now want to share the knowledge I have gathered, with more than just the people I meet in life.

Printed in Great Britain
by Amazon